MW00882748

THE LOVE BATTERY

Power Up Your Marriage for the Long Haul!

Kurt and Hollie Bryant

THE LOVE BATTERY
Power Up Your Marriage for the Long Haul

All rights reserved. No part of this publication may be reproduced, stored in a retrieval system, or transmitted in any form or by any means (electronic, mechanical, photocopy, recording, or any other), except for brief quotations in printed reviews, without prior permission of the publisher.

Copyright © 2018 by Kurt and Hollie Bryant

To our Pastors and lifetime friends, Mauricio and Virginia Ruiz, as well as Evangelists Harry and Cheryl Salem. Without your inspiration, encouragement and mentorship this book would never have been written.

CONTENTS

INTRODUCTION

The Love Battery Model

Have you noticed that any successful accomplishment typically starts with a dream? Think right now of your dream car. Imagine how nice that custom vehicle will look as it is being specially delivered to your driveway or the curb of your home. Now envision yourself sliding into the driver's seat for the first time. With excitement you turn the ignition key for the first time. Clunk. Nothing. The engine doesn't start. You have a dead battery.

It doesn't matter if your car is worth hundreds of thousands of dollars. It doesn't matter that all your car's fluids are at their proper levels, or that it is equipped with the newest state-of-the-art electronic system. It doesn't even matter if you have a full tank of gas. You're not going anywhere without a functioning power source.

Most marriages can be compared to this type of dream-gone-off-track. You get married, expecting your love for each other to take you to exciting new places in life. Over time, however, you may find yourself with little to no passion to motivate your relationship to go anywhere. Worse yet, you know your spouse probably feels the same way. Each of (what I call) your Love Batteries are very low. Worse yet, you or your spouse's battery could be dead. This is such a tragedy, especially when one or both of you lose all hope. But there is always hope. People can change. You can change. You both can begin to dream a new dream for your marriage to flourish right now!

Now back to your dream car that won't start. What if you were to call the dealer back to tell him you had a car that wouldn't work? Then you tell him you want your money back and ask him to send over someone to tow it away. The dealer replies that there is nothing wrong with the car. It just needs a battery charge. He even promises to install a new battery at no cost. Yet you insist the entire car is no good, regardless of the easy solution to bring it up and running. Would this reaction not be a tad bit insane? Amazingly that's how so many couples nowadays treat their struggling and stagnant marriages. They discount, give up on, or throw their relationship under the bus instead of considering a workable solution together to revive it.

The analogy of a car battery, given the hybrid and electric trends in the automotive industry these days, is a great analogy of what psychology calls emotional memory. In our Love Battery model, however, I want to propose to you that your joint-owned car represents your journey of love together throughout the life of your marriage. Your precious vehicle will have two batteries, each representing your unique individual ways of experiencing love. Both batteries must have at least a minimum charge for you to go anywhere in your marital relationship. Each of you should want to know how to charge the other's battery and, more importantly, how to keep it fully charged. In this series, my wife Hollie and I will discuss several ways in which you and your spouse can power up each other's Love Batteries. These Battery Boosters, as we call them, include:

1. Simple Conversation
2. Romantic Gestures
3. Regular Sex
4. Spiritual Order
5. Familial Order
6. Financial Order
7. Domestic Order
8. Nutritional & Physical Order

Consistently working the principles and tools presented in the following pages will absolutely strengthen your marriage in whatever season you find it. How can we guarantee this? Because what we present is Bible based. God says His Word will never return to Him void. It will accomplish the purpose for which He sent it (Isaiah 55:11). God wants to richly bless your marriage and He wants your marriage to bless others. He is on the side of your marriage!

All marriages need enrichment. Many need restoration. Regardless of how you view the present condition of your marriage, Hollie and I dare you and your spouse to latch hold of everything you learn in this book and own it. Sometimes what you do while you are in the process of changing for the better will seem mechanical. That's good. That means your spiritual self is rising up against your natural self to create the supernatural change you need to take your marriage to the next level. Romans 12:2 says to not be controlled by your worldly nature, but rather to be transformed by renewing your mind. If you keep pressing spiritually for your marriage, what seems to be mechanical now will become lovingly automatic over time.

United States founding father, Thomas Jefferson, is reported as having said "if you want something you've never had, you must be willing to do something you've never done." Are you ready to do some things differently in your marriage? To those of you who may have tried many things in the past that did not seem to work, I want to encourage you that God is in the business of redemption. His Word promises that He redeems and restores the souls of those who serve Him (Psalm 34:22). In the same way He can redeem the soul of your marriage if you both will trust Him and follow the wisdom of His Word, from which this teaching originates. There is no time like the present for a new start together.

Ladies and gentlemen, are you ready to start your engines? Buckle up! Let's ride!

CHAPTER ONE

Simple Conversation

"K.I.S.S. Keep it simple, stupid."

- Kelly Johnson, Aeronautical and Systems Engineer for Lockheed Corporation

How many times, and in how many situations, has this old adage proven to be the best advice? It has worked in business, finance, legal battles, politics and sports. So why do so many married couples complicate their communication between each other? Some people feel offended at the word "stupid," and have chosen to change it to "silly," but the underlying principle still rings true.

Simple, enjoyable, everyday talking (for the sake of talking) has become a lost art. So many couples today, more so than ever, miscommunicate on the fly, become frustrated, regularly argue, or get downright nasty to the point of emotionally exhausting each other. Worse yet, either a husband or wife (or both) may give up on genuine conversation with each other all together. How do we prevent this ugly downward spiral with the most important relationship we have on this earth?

One of the biggest Battery Boosters with which you can charge your spouse's Love Battery is Simple Conversation. Simple Conversation is the act of engaging in mutually satisfying everyday communication, where both parties feel understood and both are free to express themselves openly in a respectful way. With most women (and some men), Simple Conversation creates a deep emotional connection, which to them is much like a master key that unlocks the doors to all of their other major emotional needs in the relationship. That is why the development and nurturing of Simple Conversation is so vital to our marriages.

GUARD YOUR FLOW

When a spouse arrives at the point of giving up on intimate communication, almost like clockwork a third party of the opposite sex will make their appearance. They are more than willing to give a drained Love Battery a jumpstart with what seems to be totally innocent, the act of simply listening and understanding. The problem with this is that a simple conversational connection quickly meets one of the more powerful emotional needs of all human beings. Most spouses value the notion of protecting their marriage sexually, yet fail to recognize the importance of guarding their marriage conversationally. The Word of God instructs us to monitor and assess our hearts vigilantly, because from them flow fountains of life (Proverbs 4:23).

We must guard the springs of our hearts and mouths constantly; not only from what tries to flow into our hearts, but also from what wants to flow out of it. Your flow of conversation may be more emotionally refreshing to another person than you might realize. You may very well become irresistible to a troubled soul that is not your spouse. If you are conversationally starved as well, look out. You may have just set yourself up for an emotional affair (at minimum). None of us is immune to these tragic dynamics. None.

Hollie and I have ministered to many troubled couples in which one spouse had been intimately communicating with someone of the opposite sex outside of the marriage. The man or woman would be communicating by way of text or social media without their spouse's knowledge. When found out, the trust in the relationship would be severely strained or broken. Many of these messages sent would not even appear to be flirtatious or sexual in nature on a surface level, but certainly would leave their shocked husband or wife wondering about whether or not any deeper interactions may have transpired. Deep down, the offender had not been making the conversational connection at home.

HOLLIE'S HOTWIRE

"In marriage, our most intimate conversations must be reserved for our spouse only. We never want to give the devil a stick to beat us with."

UNIQUELY WIRED FOR WORDS

Men and women communicate differently in several ways. Several studies reveal that, on average, women speak more than twice the amount of words a man does in the course of a day. As a flight attendant, I have worked trips where both cabin and cockpit crew were entirely male. On one particular trip, I flew with men who spoke very little each day. At the end of the trip we expressed how great it was to work with each other. A few weeks later, a female coworker told me how she hated having flown with one of those same male flight attendants because he "barely spoke" to her the entire trip.

Don't be fooled. There are some "Chatty Chads" out there that can keep up with the best of the "Chatty Cathy's." Ask my wife. I can be one of those visionaries who, on occasion, can go on a tangent for quite a few minutes while she stares blankly at me. When I notice I have been the only one speaking for some time, I will eventually ask her if she has any perspectives on my amazing personal revelations. Inevitably she will grin and say "why, yes, about ten minutes ago I did, but you seemed so passionate. I let you ramble on. I knew you would eventually run out of steam." Thank God for Hollie. She has such tremendous patience with me and adapts so well to the eccentricities of my personality. I admit I am a recovering blabbermouth who still has occasional relapses!

"Simple Conversation is the act of engaging in mutually satisfying everyday communication, where both parties feel understood and both are free to express themselves openly in a respectful way."

Another characteristic typically unique to women is that they generally talk more for emotional connection, whereas men tend to lean more toward goal and accomplishment oriented conversation. Try sometime listening in on conversations in any public setting. Men are often the ones to try to "win" a conversation or to back up their own opinion. A man may take the perspective that he is right on a particular topic, discounting the other guy as being wrong. Women generally talk about their day to day experiences, expressing their feelings about various areas of their lives. At first glance, combining these two angles of conversation between genders may seem impossible.

Consider the frequent clashes men and women have due to these inherent conversational differences. Wives, how often have you talked to your husband about something personally distressing and his response to you is to offer practical solutions instead of simply hearing you out? How do you feel each time he does this? Husbands, how do you feel when your wife incessantly talks about her life's stressors, and yet is offended at you for offering suggestions that might help minimize (or even eliminate) these stressors?

Beyond that, think about the seemingly endless ways that our opportunities for Simple Conversation are cut off at the pass. For instance, how can you make an emotional connection with a spouse who often tunes you out at the times you really need them to pay attention? Or what if they are so touchy that they take almost everything you say personally? What if you feel so angry with your spouse that you can't seem to get back to a peaceful tone and intimately connect with them? We would all do well to carefully reflect on our interactions, in order to see what we need to change to help create a more relaxed conversational environment with our spouse.

CONVERSATIONAL SHORT CIRCUITS

Over the course of our marital relationship many of us can develop certain conversational habits that shut our spouses down emotionally, quickly draining their Love Battery. I call these Conversational Short Circuits. Oftentimes we are unaware of when we are engaging in them. We must identify these Short Circuits so we can avoid them and keep the flow of Simple Conversation going with the love of our life. James 1:19 instructs us in conversations to be swift in our hearing, slow in speaking and slow to anger. Based on this scripture, we can pinpoint at least three short circuits to Simple Conversation.

THREE COMMON CONVERSATIONAL SHORT CIRCUITS:

1. Glazing Over.

Predominantly, many of us men are guilty of not paying attention when our wives are speaking. Wives can do it too. Let's face it. After a hard day's work, we want to check out mentally. We become dull in our listening skills. As our eyes get glassy, our beloved becomes painfully aware that we are far from being swift to hear.

2. Dominating The Dojo.

Human beings talk over each other all the time. We are silently perturbed when we are the ones cut off at mid-sentence, yet justify ourselves without a fleeting thought when we do the same. One reason for this habit is our desire to drive home whatever point it is that we are making in the moment. We demand to be heard. Our fleshly minds strive to be "right." When we feel compelled to make rapid fire back-to-back points on any given topic, we will likely find ourselves dominating the conversation. It can be exhausting and irritating to our spouses when we are not slow to speak. It shuts them down.

Proverbs 18:2 says a fool could care less about fully understanding a matter, but is only passionate in expressing his own heart. In Texas, where I grew up, we say "Mamma didn't raise no fool." I don't consider myself to be a fool, so I certainly won't allow myself to act like one. I heard once from a Christian counselor that as he conversed with his wife of many decades, he would periodically tell himself silently "I am swift to hear and slow to speak." We need to be wise by listening carefully before speaking.

3. Unharnessed Anger.

When some of us think of an angry spouse, we envision verbal abuse, screaming, shoving or grabbing. However, anger can be expressed inappropriately in several other slightly less aggressive ways that are equally as painful. Anger's ugly cousins include sarcasm, the silent treatment, rolling our eyes, sighing, and (especially) a harsh tone.

Everyone feels angry at times, but the only healthy way to express anger to our spouse is to calmly say "I feel angry." After you express that you feel angry, do not let that emotion overtake you. Do not nurture the temporary pain. Otherwise you will stew in your emotions to the point of literally taking the offense to bed with you. When you do that you plant and water seeds of bitterness toward your spouse that will spring up the next day. This creates the potential for a downward spiral of senseless battery-draining arguments. The best advice for handling your anger when you feel it is found in God's word. Acknowledge that you feel angry, but do not to let your anger fester past sunset. Otherwise, you have already given Satan a foothold in your heart (Ephesians 4:26-27).

EMOJIS GONE WILD

Virginia Ruiz, Co-Lead Pastor of Elevate Church in Newhall California, teaches that the devil has absolutely no authority over a born-again believer. However, she goes on to say that the enemy takes the opportunities we give him when we let our negative emotions control us. Every time we experience a negative emotion (like anger) we have a choice to make. We will either open the door of our hearts to the devil by allowing our emotions to rule us, or we will open the door for the Holy Spirit to guide and grow us.

It is tough to push past our negative feelings. During those painful moments, why not begin to give God the opportunity to lift you up instead of giving the enemy the opportunity to bring you and your spouse down? Start dying to your pride and negativity today. You are worth it and so is your precious spouse that God gave you. In the middle of these powerful feelings, if at all possible, take a few moments alone and look at yourself in a mirror. Boldly declare before yourself, before God, and before the enemy, that by the blood of Jesus you are dead to the old person you once were and that you are a new creation in Christ! Declare that you are now putting on the new person you were designed to be, who operates only by your God-given power, love and self-control.

OTHER CONVERSATIONAL SHORT CIRCUITS:

•Expressing your way as the "right way."
•Offering solutions to your spouse's issues, instead of simply listening and understanding.
•Bringing your spouse's past failures into the present.
•Discounting your spouse's feelings.
•Playing "The Blame Game."
•Defensiveness.
•Emotionally disconnecting, or physically leaving (this is called abandonment).

One aspect that all of these Short Circuits have in common is that they are all about self. We protect self. We play emotional games to protect self. I am important as a child of God, but love is about the other person. Christ, the Groom, constantly pours out His love on His Bride (The Church). He made it about us. In response we make it about Him. In the same way, I make it about Hollie and she makes it about me. As a result, our relationship doesn't simply function. It flourishes. Yours can too.

Given that Jesus came so that you would have an abundant life, doesn't it stand to reason that you should experience an abundant marriage as well? If you will die daily to yourself and focus exclusively on charging your spouse's Love Battery (and your spouse begins to do the same), you will ultimately experience the flourishing marriage God designed you both to have. Not only do you both qualify for it, God sent His Son to die for you to have it (John 10:10).

Forget about your own needs. Make it exclusively about your spouse's needs and you will win in marriage every time. This approach goes against the grain of our worldly inclinations. Our flesh fears we will give too much and get nothing in return. In our flesh, we all lean toward emotional self-preservation. But God often tells us to do the opposite of what we have done in our stagnant past in order to get us to the place of refreshment we long to be in. Jesus said that whoever seeks to preserve his own life will ultimately lose it, but whoever loses his life for God's sake will gain a better life than he could have ever imagined. Jesus continues by speaking of the tragedy of a man gaining the whole world system, yet losing his heart in the process (Mark 8:35-36). Those words are obviously about salvation, but we can apply them to marriage as well. Hollie is my heart. I would never want to push for my way in our marriage and ultimately lose her. While reading this book, allow God to change your perspective on marriage.

SAY IT. DON'T SPRAY IT.

You might be thinking to yourself at this point about the unhealthy effects of bottled-up thoughts and emotions. I'm not talking about repressing your feelings. Sometimes it feels right when we lash out. It is not. We experience a cathartic release as a result, but it leaves our loved ones emotionally bleeding in our wake of rage. Instead, we can learn to express painful feelings in an appropriate and effective way. The Apostle Paul urged the Corinthians to be wide open because he had been wide open (2nd Corinthians 6:11-13). However, being open did not mean they were disrespectful of each other. Paul urged his fellow followers of Jesus to speak the truth, but to speak it lovingly (Ephesians 4:15). When we lovingly speak the truth, under the control of the Holy Spirit, we begin to mature in our responses to our spouse's words and behavior.

Some of you might also be thinking of the above-mentioned Unharnessed Anger as your last course of action toward a spouse that does not seem to be changing for the better. You may have even felt on occasion that your mini-tantrum or passive-aggressive action actually worked. Please do not be deceived (as I was in a previous marriage) that an occasional blast of anger toward your spouse is normal and healthy. It is not. James 1:20 assures us that our wrath doesn't bring about the results God desires. Neither does it produce the results we desire. Explosive anger births more of the same, both in yourself and in your spouse.

So how on earth can we express our discontent in a loving and productive way without short circuiting each other's Love Batteries? I'm glad you asked. I invite you now to open your heart and mind to a strategy that will enable you to express the hurt and disappointment you experience. It is a plan that works. It is a plan that will suck the defensiveness right out of the room. It is a plan that can actually facilitate emotional intimacy in the smack-dab middle of a full blown conflict.

TOOL TIME

You've heard a thousand times that we don't plan to fail. We simply fail to plan. Why not have a solid strategy for expressing those powerful feelings in an open, honest and respectful way? It is Hollie's and my joy and privilege to share with you a conversational power tool that we use almost daily in our relationship to help us stay connected. It is a phrase we use as a template to frame our feelings in order to authentically express ourselves in a way that honors each other. Are you ready for it?

Here is the magic phrase. It actually is not magical at all. On the contrary, it is very spiritual. Proverbs 16:23 declares that the wise and thoughtful in heart teaches his mouth and adds grace to the way he expresses himself. Teach your mouth to own your feelings. Respectfully express those feelings to your spouse by using the following statement:

"When you do (or say) _____, I feel _____."

This statement can be phrased in both past and present tenses. The spouse on the receiving end must accept the feeling for what it is and not take it as a personal attack.

Examples:

• "When you don't take out the trash like we agreed, I feel discounted.

• "When you were late for our date, I felt rejected."

• "When you called me a 'Big Galoot' in public, after I accidentally stomped your toe, I felt disrespected and embarrassed." (I actually said this to Hollie).

Below are several guidelines to effectively using this tool:

A. Do not use this phrase to blame, bring up the past, punish, or make assumptions about each other. Avoid "when you said that, I felt like what you were thinking was_____ " or "you made me feel___."

B. For now, do not use this phrase to attempt to resolve anything major. The main idea is to build connection, openness and honesty.

C. Accept and respect each other's feelings (whether positive or negative) in the moment. Remember to not allow yourself to take your spouse's feelings personally. Remind yourself that their feelings are simply a reaction to your words or behavior. Be empathetic and apologize often.

D. More importantly, express your feeling in only one word. Using one-word feelings will help you to own them. It is a challenge to do this, but it helps you think before speaking. When you calmly own your feelings in this manner, it is liberating. Begin to get on the same conversational page with your spouse by using this tool daily. Start now.

LOOPERS

In the 2012 Sci-Fi Thriller "Looper," a hit man's unnamed target from the future travels back through a time portal to be terminated. The hit man hesitates to follow through because he quickly identifies his target as being his future self. He was set up to literally be his own worst enemy. Upon identifying each other, they immediately begin to work together as a team to preserve their lives. Bruce Willis (the future self) understands all the weaknesses of his younger self and all the mistakes he will make. He also knows what it will take for his younger self to make a better future for himself and for those he is in relationship with.

When we get stuck on the same negative emotion, triggered by a painful past event, we become emotional loopers. We become our own worst enemies. What we believe to be a similar negative event triggers the same negative emotion over and again in similar situations, even if in reality the event is totally different. But just like Bruce Willis' character, we have the opportunity to learn from our past reactions and mistakes to have a better future. God has given us a hope and future. He knows our end from the beginning. The Holy Spirit will gladly reveal our missteps and tell us what to do to break free from being emotionally stuck. All we have to do is listen to Him and trust the guidance of His Word.

At one point in my own life, I discovered that over the years I had become increasingly agitated while driving my car. I overreacted quite frequently to passengers and other drivers. I believed Hollie was actually a horrible back seat driver, when in reality she truly was not. It became a hot button in our relationship. I humbled myself, asked Hollie's forgiveness, and proceeded to ask the Holy Spirit for His help in identifying the root of my emotional looping. God lovingly took me to a couple of stressful places in my past where I had allowed the enemy to plant two lies. Subconsciously I believed that I was a bad driver and that I had a bad sense of direction. Even though I had not had a wreck in over thirty years, I perceived almost everyone as being critical of my driving. Even though I'd driven all over the United States successfully, I believed others perceived me as geographically challenged. I forgave those that the enemy had used to instill these beliefs into me. Then I forgave myself for my knee jerk reactions.

I am now at total peace behind the wheel. To this day, sometimes I'll turn to Hollie and declare to her that I'm an excellent driver. She will giggle and agree. I love our talks in the car. It is a great place for Simple Conversation. It was a happy place I was allowing the enemy to steal from my marriage.

If we do not break our cycle of defaulting to Conversational Short Circuits, our spouse's Love Battery will be constantly drained. Conversely, we can conversationally charge up our spouse's Love Battery in at least four ways.

FOUR CONVERSATIONAL CHARGING POINTS

1. Active listening.

This is the polar opposite of passive listening. Face your spouse as often as you can when they are talking to you. Focus not only on the words they are saying, but on the feelings and thoughts behind those words. Watch their body language and facial expressions. The goal is for your spouse to know you understand and identify with what they are experiencing. One particular scientific study revealed that up to 55% of communication is body language, 38% is vocal tone, and only 7% actual words (1).

A very effective way to actively listen is to compassionately reflect back to your spouse what they are saying, but in your own words. If Hollie were to say to me, "the kitchen was a mess yesterday. I hated that my girlfriends had to see it that way. We have got to have a better plan so this will never happen again." I might respond to her with, "Baby, I am so sorry. I can see you're pretty upset. It sounds like you were embarrassed and that you want us to coordinate more on the cleaning. Am I understanding you correctly?" Speaking this way would give her the opportunity to inform me of whether or not I truly understood. If I did not, I would have the opportunity to listen more and repeat back until she knew I truly understood her. If I had responded to the same complaint with, "I'm sorry. It's just going to be that way sometimes. You know I've been working so much lately. I'll clean the kitchen when I can," then her Love Battery would have likely been short-circuited.

2. Yielding The Conversational Floor.

In order for Simple Conversation to flow, we need to allow approximately equal amounts of time for our spouses to express themselves. We also need to give our conversations a chance to breathe. When you notice you are beginning to dominate the Dojo, pause a few seconds. Then ask your spouse what their thoughts are on the topic at hand.

If you are the bigger talker in the relationship, and you find your spouse beginning to check out on the conversation, be sure to ask if you had talked over them. Ask if they were trying to say something. Be ok with silence and just being there. Allow your spouse to bring up the next topic without your prompting. Ask your spouse questions about their thoughts and feelings as they expand on the topic. You don't have to give your opinion on everything. Simply enjoy your spouse's interest in their topic.

3. Getting into their world.

Begin to learn a bit more about your spouse's interests and get them talking about it. If it is a topic that you're not that crazy about, find some aspect of it that you think you might find interesting. Ask questions about what you don't understand. Hollie worked as a transcriptionist of raw reality show footage on a TV series that highlighted America's prison systems. She enjoyed getting paid while learning about the many protocols of correctional facilities. All I had to ask her at the end of her day was "how was it in jail today?" Her eyes would light up as she told me the good, bad, ugly and hilarious moments she had witnessed on her computer screen.

4. Keeping it light.

You cannot have a positive relationship with a negative atmosphere in your home. Steer away from intensely dark conversations. Use timely and appropriate humor. Remember to converse simply for the sake of emotional connection. Carefully read and consider the wisdom of Proverbs, Chapter 17, verses 1, 22 and 27. Apply this wisdom to your daily home life immediately. Watch the overall tone in your home to ensure it is predominantly positive.

NO WALLS

Simple Conversation promotes complete and total honesty in marriage. We must respect our spouse's feelings for what they are, just feelings. Feelings are not right or wrong. They can be negative or positive. Be wide open, but don't let your emotions rule you. The idea is to get past the emotional roadblocks of negativity and back to the bliss, not to solve major conflicts each time we talk. We will cover Conflict Resolution in a later chapter.

Marriage is an earthly covenant for this life. We won't be married to each other in heaven. We will all be spiritually married to Jesus! Life is short. Make the most of it. Redeem the time. Don't waste your energy a second longer on fighting each other for control. Talk tenderly to each other. Humble yourself and do the opposite of what your fleshly mind tells you to do. Be patient with the process.

Since God hates divorce and division (Malachi 2:16), the opposite must be true. He loves a fruitful marriage. By consistently sowing positive seeds of life into your marriage with your words, you will soon begin to enjoy the fruit of what you have planted (Proverbs 18:21). When you reach that point (believe me) you will want to continue to learn, do and say what it takes to always see that spark in your spouse's eye. Wouldn't you like to get to that place? Let's keep going.

PLUG IN

1. Complete the exercise in APPENDIX A together in the back of this book. Practice using the phrase "when you do (or say), I feel" daily. Remember to use one-word feelings only. Begin to build an emotional vocabulary of both positive and negative feelings. Stop using the word "like" and the phrase "you made me feel" when expressing your feelings. Each of you start owning your own feelings. Do not take your spouse's feelings personally.

2. In pencil, fill in the Conflict Resolution Worksheet in APPENDIX B. Pick a larger hot button issue that requires a more comprehensive solution (i.e. an in-law problem, or a recurring misbehavior in one of your children). Do not compromise, or one of you will lose. Instead, resolve the conflict by combining your individual solutions into a together-solution.

3. Identify each of your top Conversational Short Circuits when conversing with your spouse (i.e. Dominating the Dojo, Unharnessed Anger). Begin to recognize when you do them. Begin to spiritually die to these habits (Romans 6:11). Also share one Conversational Charging Point your spouse does that helps you to feel loved (i.e. Getting Into Their World, Yielding the Floor). Share with each other which specific Charging Points you would like to be injected into your conversations immediately. Start today.

NOTES

1. Mehrabian, A., & Ferris, S. R. (1967). Inference of attitudes from nonverbal communication in two channels, Journal of Consulting Psychology 31(3), 248-252.

ZAPPLICATION NOTES

(If something in the reading caught your attention and "zapped" you with a personal revelation, this is the place to jot it down for immediate life application)

CHAPTER TWO

Romantic Gestures

"Happiness in marriage is not something that just happens. A good marriage must be created. The courtship should not end with the honeymoon. It should continue through the years."

- Paul Newman, the day he married JoAnn Woodward

Actor, Entrepreneur and Philanthropist Paul Newman was happily married to JoAnn Woodward for 50 years until his death in 2008. Their fulfilling marriage was an anomaly, to say the least, in the midst of a martially divided Hollywood crowd of revolving celebrity relationships. The Newmans nurtured their relationship with romance throughout the life of their marriage.

My father, Dr. James Bryant, romanced my mother for the 54 years of their thriving marriage. In 2014, two weeks into his recovery from open chest surgery, mom stooped down to tie his shoe. She said, "this is how I say I love you." Leaning forward, he kissed her forehead and responded, "and that's how I say I love you." Shortly afterward, dad died suddenly of a pulmonary embolism. Some of the last words he said to the love of his life were those of affection and romance. Those tender words, along with the accompanying action, characterized the heart of a well-nurtured marriage of many decades.

All the way up to the month of his death, dad would have a weekly date night with mom. Almost every Friday evening I would get a call from him with a personal review of the movie they had just seen. Once per year, he would take a vacation with her. Over the years, they flew all over the world together and took a few cruises as well.

A few years ago my friend, Evangelist Harry Salem, asked me candidly "why on earth would you get married a third time?" I knew he did not mean anything personal. He knew I was having an amazing relationship with Hollie and that together we ran a second-to-none marriage ministry at our church. I was stumped at that moment for an answer to his question, but reflected later on the fact that it was because my parents had kept their romantic flame burning for so long. Because of their flourishing marriage, I knew deep down that somehow marriages worked. As parents, the biggest gift you can give to your children is staying madly in love with each other. Your marriage will affect their future marriage in a more profound way than you could ever imagine.

POUR IT ON

Romantic Gestures are affectionate acts that demonstrate care and promote emotional connection. Ways of extending this highly necessary emotional need are virtuously endless. These gestures are packaged in numerous forms (with endless variations), from flirting, to cards, to gifts, to bed etiquette and everything in between.

When the Apostle Paul instructs men and women to not withhold affection from each other, except for periods of prayer and fasting, he is referring specifically to sexual relations. He goes on to say that a husband's body belongs to his wife and the wife's body to the husband. However, romance is a necessary component most of the time for almost all women to be fully satisfied in their sex life.

At times wives can feel taken for granted if their husbands fail to help them feel special prior to lovemaking. If a man consistently meets his wife's need for romantic affection, I believe he fulfills this scripture more completely. Romance in marriage can be viewed as an overall covering, like a tent. Sex would be the "event within the tent." Husbands would do well to see the romance they experience with their wives in this fashion, focusing more on the tent than on the event.

"Romantic Gestures are affectionate acts that demonstrate care and promote emotional connection."

Romance has proven to be such a powerful need for women, so much so that lucrative Soap Opera Television series have stood the test of time for many decades. The same can be said of the Romance Novel literary genre. An elderly woman on a flight I was working was engaged in one of these sultry reads. She had the letters of her electronic reader enlarged to such gigantic font, that I had to turn my head every time I passed her row to avoid seeing the erotic rhetoric. Had there been unaccompanied minors near her, I would have had to reseat them in a different part of the cabin!

TOUCHY FEELY

In modern day American culture it is now socially acceptable in any number of situations for men and women, who have absolutely no romantic connection, to casually embrace each other. After a great working trip together, some flight crewmembers will give each other a quick benign hug. When I lived in Costa Rica in the Eighties, it was very common for women and men that knew each other to greet each other with a peck on the cheek. The kiss was so light it was like almost kissing the air. However, if someone had not known you for long and you kissed a little too close to the corner of their mouth (or for too long), they would think you had ulterior motives. All cultures have boundaries when it comes to what is perceived as a romantic display.

Given the power that Romantic Gestures can potentially wield, we are wise to guard ourselves from crossing boundaries. Some of you may contend that it is your nature to touch just about anyone, regardless of gender, because you don't mean anything by it. Nevertheless, just as with our private Regular Conversation, our touches can trigger an emotional chain reaction with someone who is starved for romance. Even a glance or a wink can boost a drained love battery.

If someone of the opposite sex wants to touch you too frequently, or in ways you are not comfortable with, avoid physical contact with them in anyway you can. A female passenger came to the back of the aircraft one time to converse with me and my crew. She could tell we were all tired and had had a long day. Without asking permission, one by one, she began to rub each of the flight attendants neck and shoulders. It was obvious she had been trained in massage therapy. When she came up behind me, I recoiled from her. Seeing that she was offended, I told her that I only let my wife give me massages. She said that her touch was spiritual and that good energy flowed through her hands, causing her to feel good in the process. All the more reason, I thought to myself, to have not allowed her to touch me.

In our church's marriage enrichment groups, we have taught couples to guard their marriage by embracing only dear friends or relatives. As for every other opposite sex friend we are close to, we extend the "side hug." Female friends at work and church, who I have known for years, sometimes chuckle at the fact that I have become the "Master Side Hugger."

Another safeguard is to not flirt with anyone except our spouses. If we are not flirting regularly in marriage, we need to begin (or restart) the habit of flirting. Subtle flirting is a way to stay romantically connected to your spouse in a public place, whether it's by playing footsie under a table or winking from across a crowded room. Hollie and I often flirt when we text or email each other. Sometimes a few tender emojis are all it takes to top off her Love Battery. No one else receives the particular emojis I send her. They are meant exclusively for her, and her alone. It may not seem very theological, but I could imagine the Apostle Paul on present day social media. He might very well instruct married couples to not withhold the emojis that are due their husband or wife!

WHEN IN DOUBT, TALK IT OUT

There are countless books and magazine articles that instruct men and women on how to try new methods of romancing our one and only. I am not going to do that in this book. You don't need a list of 101 ways to spark a romantic flame. The Bible says when a couple marries that they become one flesh. You already know the Romantic Gestures your spouse needs. Some of us may think we have forgotten, but deep down we still know. If we feel we don't know, we should ask the expert on exactly what our spouse needs. That expert is your spouse. Get a conversation going. Jot down a few notes.

One great part about communicating your specific romantic desires to your mate is that it takes the guesswork out of it for them. As a result, you get romanced in the way that you want. When you were dating, you threw romantic acts out there like spaghetti against a wall. You wanted to see what would stick. Back then it didn't matter. You were getting to know each other. Any effort to be romantic was appreciated. That's the main reason why some men will continue to demonstrate certain acts of affection from "back in the day" that no longer connect with their wives.

A major benefit of verbalizing the ways we feel romanced is that of enjoying the seasons of personal change. King Solomon said that everything has its season (Ecclesiastes 3:1). Enjoy the seasons of your romantic lives together. Roll with them. My mother teaches the marital principle of "I change. You change. We change." For example, one of you stops liking green peas on Thursdays. Consequently, the other of you stops cooking green peas on Thursdays. So what happens the following Thursday? You eat asparagus. The same applies to Romantic Gestures. Let's say you've been going out to the movies together most Friday nights for the past three years. One of you stops enjoying it. For the next two months you agree to have dinner delivered and watch a TV series while you cuddle each other on the couch.

Having a weekly date inside your home doesn't sound romantic to some couples, but to others it does. Just because you see your married friends on social media zip lining across South America doesn't necessarily mean you're less romantic by being lower key in this season of your lives together. The key is to plan for times and places for spontaneous romance to occur. It does not have to be expensive, but it does have to be consistent.

ROMANTIC SHORT CIRCUITS

I once heard a flight attendant colleague of mine conclude her detailed safety announcement by stating "basically, folks, remember to do the do the do's and don't do the don'ts." Let's discuss some of the don'ts of romance that result in Romantic Short Circuits.

Examples:

1. Forgetting significant dates and events.
2. Expecting that your spouse should already know what you are wanting (or thinking) in the moment.
3. Husbands not opening the door for wives.
4. Rough tone.
5. Impatience.
6. Forgetting to minimize distractions during your private time together. (phone, texts, social media).
7. Attempting to meet our spouse's previously expressed needs on our terms, and not in a way that helps them feel valued.

Actions and inactions like these will obviously suck the life out of your potential romantic moments. A combination of a few of these, over time, could create a relational backdrop of disappointment. Continued disappointment eventually leads to emotional disconnection. An extremely low Love Battery is vulnerable to a charge from an outside source.

For those who might be recovering from the wounds of infidelity, what has just been stated may not seem fair at all. At the same time, those who have been unfaithful cannot use emotional disconnection as an excuse for an any type of affair. Both husband and wife must be transparent about how their individual Love Batteries are specifically charged. We are wise to gauge how loved our spouse's feel at any given time during the week. We need input, for better or for worse, as to how well we are helping them feel connected to us. Our marriages cannot afford for either one of us to be defensive, particularly when it comes to the romantic course corrections needed to help our intimacy flourish. Die to your pride and love your lover the way they want to be loved.

When I sense Hollie's Love Battery is a little low, I will ask her what she needs for me to do that would fully charge it. Many times she will simply answer "be sweet to me." She knows I already know how to romance her in the ways she likes, because I pursued her with the same types of Romantic Gestures during our courtship. We also periodically discuss our likes and dislikes, when it comes to meeting each other's romantic needs.

Reactivate the romantic areas of your Love Batteries. Change things up a bit to enhance the atmosphere. For example, instead of the usual dinner and a movie, try a "movie and a dinner." Go to the matinee first, then you can discuss the flick over sushi and be back home for some more intimate activity. A little planning goes a long way.

It is time to put our thinking caps on and get some fresh romantic vision. You can do it. God designed you both to take each other's breath away for as long as you have breath in your lungs. So take a deep breath and go for it! Since marriage represents God's Kingdom, all of heaven cheers you on!

PLUG IN

1. Complete the exercises in APPENDICES C, D, E, and F. Plan a weekly date night without the children. Put the dates into your family calendar. Discuss with each other ahead of time what it is you both would like to do on your dates. Guard your time together. Be sure to avoid Romantic Short Circuits. Inject your spouse's top Romantic Charging Points into your date nights. Also begin to plan your annual family vacations and "just the two of us" vacations.

2. If by this point, having practiced the tools in this book, you feel as though you do not have the ability to give or receive love, consider the possibility that you have either strayed away from God, or maybe even need to be equipped with a new Love Battery. Only God can give you this gift. It is absolutely free. If you do not have a personal relationship with God through Jesus, Hollie and I encourage you to invite Him into your heart and life right now.

Pray "God, thank You for paying the price for my failures and mistakes through Your Son Jesus' death. I ask that Your Spirit would come into my spirit at this moment so I experience a new life filled with Your love and power. I freely yield to You to call the shots in my life. In Jesus' name I pray. Amen."

3. If you prayed this prayer for the first time you are now what Jesus calls reborn. If you have either been reborn or given your life back to Jesus let us know by email at thelovebattery@gmail.com of your new relationship with God. We want to celebrate you and agree in prayer for anything you need. Congratulations! You now have the added advantage of personally powering up on God's unconditional love, which you can then extend to your spouse.

ZAPPLICATION NOTES

CHAPTER THREE

Regular Sex

"Let's talk about sex, baby. Let's talk about you and me. Let's talk about all the good things and the bad things that may be."

- Salt-n-Pepa, "Let's Talk About Sex." Blacks' Magic album, 1990.

This tune obviously does not carry all wholesome lyrics in its entirety. In no way am I promoting the song. However, the chorus stresses the importance and benefits of talking more about sex.

Certainly parents need to share with their adolescent children the pitfalls of premarital sex and the rewards of celibacy before marriage. However, it is equally important that husbands and wives regularly communicate with each other about their own personal sex life together. All too often many do not, ending up dissatisfied for years on end. Much like a wife who is starved in the areas of Simple Conversation and Romantic Gestures, a sexually deflated husband can begin to shut down in other areas of emotional need-meeting. Receiving a regular sexual power boost from his one-and-only can motivate him to more passionately meet her top Battery Boosters.

It is important to discover each other's erotic zones and what atmosphere each spouse needs when under the bed sheets. The more you talk about what you like, the more you will understand each other's sexual goals and objectives. That's right. Married couples should have sexual strategies together to make sure this vital need is regularly met in a way that is pleasing to both husband and wife. Sex should be entered into on a consistent basis. That is why we have chosen to refer to this particular Battery Booster as Regular Sex. Regular Sex is for the life of the marriage. It is a beautiful wedding gift from God.

HOLLIE'S HOTWIRE:
"A wife needs to clearly communicate to her husband what satisfies her sexually."

THE PERKS

There are many mental, relational, emotional and physiological benefits to having regular sex. Frequency can be hotly debated. However, the positive results of regularly satisfying each other's sexual desire are clearly evident.

One very important result of ongoing marital sex is that it guards the marriage. The Apostle Paul advises in 1st Corinthians 7:3 that husbands and wives should freely and regularly demonstrate their affection to one another. He proceeds to answer as to why in verse 5 of the same chapter for us not to not stop showing each other affection, except when we are in a brief season of fasting and praying. If we do not return to intimacy quickly, we are vulnerable to the temptation to lust.

Some of those who have been unfaithful in marriage misapply this scripture to justify their own unholy actions, pinning the blame on their spouse for their own lack of control. How shameful and cruel is that? James 1:14-16 explains the incubation and manifestation process of all sin, including infidelity. Temptation presents itself when the tempted stirs up their own fleshly desires. This creates an environment for sin to be nurtured and birthed. We all must take personal responsibility for our own actions.

At the same time, we must acknowledge the general fact that most men desire sex more often than most women. According to an Ohio State University research on how often college-aged students think about sex, data revealed that a man has close to 19 sexual thoughts per day to a woman's 10 thoughts (1). Men may think of sex up to twice as much as women do. Quite frankly, I personally believe that on many days I am above this statistic. I may be middle-aged, but I'm not dead!

Regular Sex is such a powerful need that it often ranks as the number one Battery Booster for a husband. When his need is not met consistently it makes it all the more difficult for him to control his eyes, which have a fleshly tendency to wander. A wise woman will recognize this and satisfy her man regularly. A wise man will satisfy his wife each time in the process (or at least offer to). This leaves both husband and wife wanting to come back for more. Fulfilled desire promotes continued desire, which minimizes straying desire.

Fulfilled desire promotes continued desire, which minimizes straying desire.

Numerous scientific studies agree that sex (at least twice per week) helps husbands and wives to stay healthier and more vibrant in many ways. As a result of regular sex, we generate higher levels of a unique blood protein which fights off viruses at their onset. Husbands become almost half as likely to develop heart disease. We both can experience a better stress response, resulting in lower overall blood pressure. We obviously burn a few calories each time we make love. We also build better overall muscle tone. Sex can serve as significant pain relief to arthritis, headache, leg pain and back pain. It can even minimize a woman's menstrual cramps. Regular Sex also helps a wife to increase her production of vaginal moisture and blood flow, which ultimately helps her to better enjoy sex and to crave it more often.

Many evangelists and Christian medical professionals currently express their excitement in watching how secular science has begun to parallel biblical teachings in both nature and mankind. Several studies reveal that regular sex sets the stage for increased levels of oxytocin, a hormone that contributes to feelings of empathy and emotional bonding. The Bible describes this experience as two becoming one in flesh (Genesis 2:24). The word flesh does not only refer to our physical bodies. It includes our thoughts and emotions as well.

CLOSED FOR BUSINESS

With all the overwhelming biblical and scientific evidence as to the benefits of making love regularly, why is sexual frequency diminishing so drastically in so many marriages? Why do so many spouses give up on something God meant to be so special? Remember that it is His plan (according to His Word) that married couples engage in lovemaking on a regular basis. So why is it that sex in so many marriages has come to a screeching halt? Let's examine several causes.

Cultural influence plays a significant role in how sex in marriage is often viewed. For example, think of the typical secular Bachelor and Bachelorette parties on the eve prior to countless weddings in Western culture. Premarital sex is celebrated and marital sexual exclusivity mourned, as groomsmen hire strippers to tantalize the groom one final time before he takes the plunge of being tied down to one woman. In a great way, this type of behavior speaks death over a married couple's sex life before it even begins. Some may react to what I just expressed, scoffing "give me a break, Kurt. It's just all in fun. It's a tradition." But everything you do and say has meaning. The Word of God says that life and death are empowered by our words (Proverbs 18:21). If you speak positively about your sex life you will reap the reward.

Why not celebrate the new season that brides and grooms are stepping into. Don't get drunk. Some of the most memorable events you can bless a husband or wife-to-be prior to taking their vows can take place at a restaurant, movie theater, bowling alley, or even a shooting range. At some point during the event make a non-alcoholic toast and speak life and blessing over their future together. They will never forget it. After all, haven't they both found the good thing the Bible speaks of in Proverbs 18:20?

HEAR NO EVIL, SEE NO EVIL, SPEAK NO EVIL

Television, movies and social media in recent decades have also projected the idea of sex ending after marriage. Many couples live together thinking the full commitment of marriage would be a curse to their special relationship. This perception of marriage as ultimately ending up sexless is often presented as the norm. Many of the general public are fascinated upon hearing stories of elderly couples making love on a regular basis. I have a Urologist friend who knows men who are well into their nineties that have sex twice per month on average.

Pornography is another sex killer in marriage. Jesus said that if a man looks at a woman in a lustful way, he has already committed adultery with her on a heart level (Matthew 5:28). Since adultery is sin, and the wages of sin is death (Romans 6:23), then it stands to reason that the sex life of a porn-infested marriage will soon die. If a husband is filling his heart with adulterous fantasies he is quickly pushing the love he has for his wife out of his heart. Global pornography revenues are currently approaching 100 billion dollars. It has become a major addiction for men, and nowadays for more and more women. This industry could care less about the pain and damage it inflicts on marriages worldwide.

Pornography contributes to marital mistrust, as it is typically viewed secretly. This goes against the grain of a successful marriage, which is based in great part on honesty and openness. Porno storylines almost always carry themes of deception that are downloaded into the viewer's mind. Sights and sounds are enhanced and exaggerated. As a result of regular viewing, a porn-addicted husband will eventually project unrealistic sexual expectations onto his wife. He soon experiences dissatisfaction and is drawn into more porn. Subconsciously he will begin to view his wife (and women in general) as objects intended for his selfish sexual satisfaction. Consequently a wife will feel rejected, abandoned and resentful.

41

Most all men have struggled with pornography at some point in their lives. As a Christian man, you must stop "coping" with porn and be free from it. Your wife is worth it. So are you. A great book to help you form a victorious strategy to guard against lust is Every Man's Battle. A great passage of scripture with which to combat this sin is Romans 6. This chapter states that believers in Christ are dead to their sinful deeds and alive to God's ways (Romans 6:11). When you start to regularly die to the sin of lust, that's when you will become free of it. Run from lust (1st Corinthians 6:18). Turn off your computer and smartphone at an early hour of the evening. Stop channel-surfing on your TV. Soft porn leads rapidly to hard porn. Get radical. As you cut off your electronics, point at them and say "I am dead to you, lust, by the blood of Jesus." Don't give yourself an excuse of any kind to relapse. Repentance means you don't look back. Men, talk with a trusted brother in Christ who has victory in this area. Get your eyes of love (not lust) back on the wife of your youth. Let her be the only one to satisfy you (Proverbs 5:19).

BITTER PILLS WE SWALLOW

Hollie says a husband's biggest battle to conquer is his lust, and a woman's biggest battle is her bitterness. Unresolved childhood abuse or deep relational wounds (especially from her husband) can shut down a wife's desire for sex like nothing else. My Pastor, Mauricio Ruiz, says that one's wound can become their weapon. Then everyone around them suffers.

God says to actively seek to be at peace with all people, and to live a holy lifestyle, without which we will not experience the things of the Lord. In addition, we must examine our hearts and lives so we don't fall short of God's grace. By taking this approach we keep bitterness from taking root in our hearts. Bitter roots result in chaotic relationships (Hebrews 12:14-15). Meditate on that for a moment. When a wounded person stops pursuing peace with their spouse, it short-circuits their own personal relationship with God. They can't seem to hear from The Holy Spirit like they did before. By holding on to unforgiveness they sever themselves from the favor they once received from God. Their misery becomes a contagion that affects every family member and friend around them. What's worse is that the one who has the deepest root of bitterness is the one who is most deeply rooted in denial. They perceive their spouse as the one who has "made them miserable." However (as a side note), if you are experiencing abuse, get out. In this case your spouse IS the problem. Your body is a temple of the Holy Spirit, not a punching bag.

Those who hold fast to a victim mentality in marriage may actually use the withholding of sex as a weapon, claiming they cannot give themselves freely to the one who has so deeply hurt them emotionally. The other spouse's sexual need is then left hanging out to dry. This is not love. True love forgives, keeping no record of the other's wrong toward us (1st Corinthians 13:5b). That's not to say there won't be wounded emotions to be healed or trust that needs to be restored along the way. No matter how angry Hollie may be with me, she will never hold back sex. That is humbling for me. I don't take that kind of love for granted. That kind of love inspires me to work on what I need to in order for her not to feel hurt. I always strive for us to be at peace, and for her Love Battery to be fully charged.

A man's libido can be affected by emotional pain as well. A wife's sex drive tends to be more connected to her feelings of intimacy, whereas a husband's sex drive is more interconnected with his feelings of being respected by his wife. The idea that a man will never turn down sex is not entirely true. If he has felt belittled in some way, he can be the one who will hold back in the bedroom. Husbands need to drop their pride and calmly communicate their feelings. Refer back to the tool from Simple Conversation "when you do/say_____, I feel_____ (i.e. disrespected, degraded, etc.)." These types of feelings are difficult for a man to express. If a wife accepts those feelings, her husband's inner love tiger will soon emerge!

If your sex life is suffering in marriage because you're holding back, ask the Holy Spirit to help you identify any root of bitterness. Once you see it, you have the ability to pull it out. A great guide to help you with this process is the book The Bait of Satan by John Bevere. If I had not identified the roots of bitterness I had planted in my heart from past broken relationships, and had not pulled them out years ago, I would have carried those weed-like wounds into my marriage with Hollie and ruined it. When you truly understand forgiveness, and are free from your prison of bitterness, you will begin to receive God's love again and give your body freely to your spouse.

I GUESS THAT'S WHY THEY CALL IT THE BLUES

Chronic depression can slowly drain a Love Battery, wreaking havoc on a couple's sex life. Many years ago I was medically diagnosed with severe depression and Generalized Anxiety. For the four years that followed I was on and off antidepressants. I would feel great when I was on the meds, then nosedive emotionally when I was off of them. Having gathered quite a bit of psychological information in the course of treatment, I read many sources that agreed that almost all depression was treatable through therapy without medication. My doctor incrementally stepped me off of (what I determined) would be my last round of Paxil. I went through a 12-week Men's group at a local church, which facilitated my inner healing. The group curriculum included the book Changes That Heal, by Dr. Henry Cloud. I later worked some exercises I had learned from various books, including The Battlefield of the Mind (Joyce Meyer) and Your Best Life Now (Joel Osteen). I resolved within myself that I would be hurting for awhile, while I dealt with what was generating my pain. I was done with emotional band-aids. I wanted solutions that worked.

Depression is a dark spiritual bondage to negative mindsets. One believes lies about themselves, God, others and personal circumstances. To break free from depression, an individual has to identify and pull down negative thought patterns. They must also intentionally replace that negativity with positive, true thoughts. Your pastor can refer you to Bible-based resources and licensed counselors (if needed) to help you with this process.

Confessing personalized scripture out loud has transformed my thinking and emotions. Through speaking God's Word into my life and leaning on God's loving presence, I became totally free from the stranglehold of depression. Staying connected to my church helped as well. The Word of God promises that when you plant yourself in

His house, your life will flourish (Psalm 92:13). When you are serving others, it gets your mind off of you. When you have been depressed, you have been self absorbed. Evangelist Cheryl Salem says depression is ultimately rooted in pride. She says a "poor old me" attitude still boils down to making it about all about "me."

Personal worship also helped lift me from the muck and mire of depression. God says when we feel heavy-hearted we should put on the robe of praise (Isaiah 61:3). Hollie and I guard our hearts from gloominess and negativity by putting on Pandora or YouTube Christian music channels. We praise and worship God together for a few minutes, just as if we were in church. Soon the heaviness evaporates and the Holy Spirit downloads to us a fresh spiritual perspective. To be completely authentic, many times we feel so free we end up in the bedroom for a romp in the hay!

Some depression is a normal part of grieving a loss, like with the death of a dear family member. Mourning, however, should not be a crippling malady that lasts for years. A must-read for anyone who has suffered a tragic loss is From Mourning To Morning, by Cheryl and Harry Salem.

Sex can help a depressed or grieving spouse on the mend. All the natural feel-good chemicals and hormones are released at orgasm, including oxytocin and endorphins. A pastor friend of mine lost his father suddenly. After the funeral, his wife asked him privately if there were anything she could do to ease his suffering. He immediately blurted out "I need sex!"

The most common issue that chokes out sex in marriage is a lack of order and priorities. In our many years of marriage ministry, Hollie and I have observed countless couples who no longer live life. They are essentially "being lived." Many put their children first before the marriage. I always tell couples that the biggest gift they can give their children is the assurance that mommy and daddy are doing what it takes to stay madly in love with each other. This instills deep-down confidence in children that marriage can be (and should be) successful. The love that continually happens behind your bedroom doors will result in an afterglow that will bless your children's marital future.

PARTY PLANNING

If we have no specific plan for our sexual needs to be fulfilled, this need will be pushed aside and unmet. Starved needs will always cause a marriage to suffer. Many couples we have ministered to are of the opinion that good sex must be spontaneous. Consider the following scenario. Does a great experience at an amusement park happen spontaneously? What if I suddenly announced to Hollie on a workday "let's be spontaneous and go right now to Disneyland!" She would want to go but not be able to. Then what if I said to her "I am so disappointed! We haven't been there in years! We'll never get there ever again!" That would not be fair at all, mainly to her. After all, she loves Disneyland even more than I do. Wouldn't she want us rather to plan regular outings to "the happiest place on earth?" Would the times we scheduled to spend time there not be as exciting as if they had been spur-of-the-moment? Could there not be spontaneous, unforgettable moments that would happen within the hours that we had planned to be there? That's the whole point for scheduling time for enjoyable activities. The same principle holds true with our sex lives. Sexual spontaneity thrives within the timeframe you both have created.

A wonderful thing about marriage is that you both bought the season pass to sexual fulfillment when you said "I do." Now it is simply a matter of planning regular times to allow for those special moments to occur. If you don't plan, you miss out. It is guaranteed that one of you will be more disappointed than the other.

Get a vision together of how great a regular sex life will be for your marriage. The Bible says to then write that vision down and make it clear (Habakkuk 2:2). Consider entering the dates and hours into your weekly calendar. If it's written down, you'll be the ones who read it and run with it. This will give you something to look forward to regularly. As you take a few minutes to schedule your month together, be realistic about what times work best for you. Get creative. Perhaps put an agreed-upon emoticon or symbol on the days of the week and the hour that you plan to make love. If something comes up that is out of your control, for example on an evening you have scheduled for sex, do it the next morning. If once in awhile it does not happen at the time you have planned, at least you will know that you had it planned. At least you are having more sex. At least it's happening on a regular basis. Not having a plan is a plan for failure.

HOLLIE'S HOTWIRE:
"Not scheduling sex is an excuse for avoiding a vital part of your marriage. The fruit of not scheduling sex will ultimately be a sexless marriage."

KEEP ON KEEPING ON

For a field to produce the expected crop it must be cultivated. It is much of the same process when we begin new intimate habits with our spouse. We must make preparations, as well as nurture our sex lives along the way, in order for mutual satisfaction to grow and to keep growing.

We must both cultivate sexual consistency. For a man, consistency is experienced in the form of frequency. In the 1998 movie Six Days Seven Nights, Harrison Ford's character explains the way a woman gets a man aroused. He says simply "she shows up." Wives, make lovemaking a priority and simply show up. Your husband desires you, no matter what state you're in. Make love at least twice per week. When you are tired, try doing it anyway. The enemy is the one who wants you to have less sex. Why not put it in his face by enjoying each other instead of giving up. Some of the most amazing sex you can have is when you are exhausted. That is because your mind is checked out and your body has a chance to release its stress in the process.

A husband needs to cultivate sexual desire in his wife through regular non-sexual affection. Activities like frequent hugs, holding hands, and embracing each other while relaxing all help to create an environment where a wife can enjoy sex more. Affection can be viewed as an emotional tent for her. In this context, sex would be the event within the tent. Typically a wife can release herself sexually when she trusts her husband to help create a lovingly affectionate environment she can rest in. Men, be sure not to poke holes in this tent with actions you know she does not enjoy. Belching the alphabet (guilty as charged) or a game of grabby-grab may be fun for you, but most likely could be a major short-circuit to her Love Battery.

GOING THE DISTANCE

In Amsterdam, on October of 2007, an international panel of 21 scientific experts in the field of premature ejaculation convened to write a definition of it. After reviewing much research they determined that "premature ejaculation is a male sexual dysfunction characterized by ejaculation which always (or nearly always) occurs prior to, or within about, one minute of vaginal penetration; and, inability to delay ejaculation on all (or nearly all) vaginal penetrations; and, negative personal consequences, such as distress, bother, frustration, and/or the avoidance of sexual intimacy (2)." With all due respect to the scientific community on this topic, I sincerely ask "who cares?!" Seriously. Why the stigma of a quicker-than-desired sexual response as being dysfunctional. If both husband and wife are satisfied at some point during love making, neither need be concerned that their sex life is doomed. Granted (back to the Disneyland analogy) a man may very well want the ride to last longer. Perhaps one of your goals together might be an increased stroke count. This is fine. However, my contention is that we should leave the performance trap out of the bedroom.

PE, as it is now called, when googled reveals endless articles, studies and remedies for what Western Culture now deems as tragically substandard. If a man believes his rapid sexual response to be abnormal, he may grow more anxious each time it occurs. The anxiety of it all could lead him to regularly experience a quick climax as a result of a self-fulfilling prophecy! Women are not typically obsessed with sexual performance as much as men are. Husband, it's time to dump this worldly view of orgasm, command out fear, and enjoy yourself. Your wife wants you to enjoy yourself. She wants to enjoy you.

Now that you (husband) have hopefully ceased from labeling yourself as a walking disorder, let's talk about increasing your time in the saddle. Many Legalistic Christians would want to shut down this specific topic of interest. They might label it as being ungodly. I would argue that sex in a Christian marriage should be flourishingly satisfying for both husband and wife. After all, Jesus said He came to give us life more abundant (John 10:10). Shouldn't that apply to the delightful act that God designed to be exclusive to the marriage bed?

We don't have to get raunchy in order to explain the mechanics of sex, nor should we. As a warning, I strongly I advise you to stay away from graphic sexual instruction videos and graphic sex manuals. By watching another couple make love, you will spiritually invite them into your sex life. Just like with staged pornography, you will have burned their images into your mind. However, reading about non-promiscuous techniques can prove very helpful. Even at that, limit how much of these articles you read. Learn a few things you can use that you are both in agreement with. The more important thing is that you learn from each other as to what pleases each other.

A man can last longer in several ways. Two keys for a man to attain ejaculatory control are to maintain a relaxed pelvic area and to regulate his breathing. If a husband is on top, lunging away with his hips and breathing heavily, he will soon reach the point of inevitability and it will all be over. Gravity plays a part as well, in terms of where his semen originates and the direction of its flow. To be more specific, a man's PC muscle (the same muscle that holds back urine) has a slightly more challenging time holding back semen when he is on top.

Two keys for a man to attain ejaculatory control are to maintain a relaxed pelvic area and to regulate his breathing.

Wife, if your husband desires to amplify his enjoyment of sex by learning to delay his ejaculation, it may be more productive for you to be on top for a season. If this position truly does not appeal to you, consider buying a bed that is at the height of your husband's standing crotch level. Husband, before you start making it all about you and do your happy dance, may I highly suggest that each time you make love that you first offer to bring your wife to an orgasm. This can be done digitally, orally, or through a simultaneous combination of both. Husbands need to let wives patiently teach them how to help them climax and wives need to assertively speak up. Most women have a craving for sex on average twice per month. So she may not always want it. Let's debunk the myth right now that a woman has to reach orgasm every time she makes love in order to enjoy herself. This is simply not true.

The beauty of stimulating your wife to orgasm first is that afterwards it really doesn't matter how long you last. The pressure is off. You can go quickly, or begin to practice delaying your ejaculation. With your wife on top, let your pelvic area completely relax. Let her move, not you. Take gentle, prolonged, slow belly breaths in and out. Inhale slowly for about two or three seconds. Exhale slowly for three to four seconds until your lungs are almost empty. Remember that heavier breathing leads you more quickly to ejaculation. Slower, controlled breathing helps you to slow your response.

A pastor friend of mine once said to a group of married men that he had a clock on his bedroom nightstand. The only reason for this clock was for him to look at it periodically during sex, because he had learned his wife typically climaxed after twelve minutes. While a man relaxes and enjoys lovemaking, he can count minutes or strokes (silently, of course!). Maybe you lasted seven minutes the first time. The next time you last nine. After a month you last fifteen to twenty minutes. If you take the silent counting approach, let's say you reach 100 strokes within a couple of weeks. After a few months you work up to 500 strokes. One day you discover you can last as long as you want to and your wife has an orgasm. With your newfound control, you can then be more confident in other positions.

HURDLES

Numerous medical and aging issues can challenge your sex life. These include sleep apnea, menopause, diabetes, neurological damage, and spinal cord injury. Do whatever it takes together to overcome these obstacles and you will succeed. Don't give up. Get creative. Seek medical advice. Don't get religiously legalistic about doctors. The author of the third book of the New Testament was a physician. If you need a CPAP machine, hormones, Viagra, or genital surgery, then you should consider it. You are worth it and so is your spouse.

Regular Sex is meant for the life of the marriage. Boost your spouse's Love Battery with it often. It will take you to places of enjoyment you might not have expected.

PLUG IN

1. Take the Regular Sex Pop Quiz in APPENDIX G. Review this chapter briefly to find the correct answers to the questions you answered incorrectly.

2. Both you and your spouse write down one or two personal sexual goals and discuss them together. Formulate a plan together to reach these goals.

3. Schedule the two times per week you will make love. Enter them into your family calendar. If you already are making love twice per week add another "do it" day to your schedule.

4. Just do it!

Notes:

1. Fisher, T. D., Moore, Z. T. & Pittenger, M. (2012). Sex on the Brain. Journal of Sex Research, pages 29, 69-77. DOI: 10.1080/00224499.2011.565429.

2. International Society for Sexual Medicine (2007). Definition of Premature Ejaculation (PE), www.issm.info (ISSM Executive Office, P.O. Box 94, 1520 AB Wormerveer, The Netherlands).

ZAPPLICATION NOTES

CHAPTER FOUR

Relational Order

Do everything in a godly and orderly fashion.

- 1st Corinthians 14:40 (paraphrased by authors)

If you and your spouse owned a debt-free twenty million dollar mansion that had each room filled to the ceiling with horse manure, what would you do? Would you give up and abandon it? Would you sell it to an investor for pennies on the dollar? Would you have it demolished? These questions may sound odd, but stick with me for a minute.

The Bible says that through wisdom a house is built, by understanding it is established, and that through knowledge its rooms are filled with pleasant and precious treasures (Proverbs 24:3-4). I believe we can apply this process to the building of a life together as husband and wife. We can also apply this principle to the reordering of a marriage that has gone off track.

By the way, the wisest answer to the above scenario would be to clean out your home one room at a time, then renovate. Would that be costly and stinky along the way? Absolutely. Would it take careful planning and extreme patience? Of course the bottom line is that if the foundation is solid and the basic structure is intact, your home remains a valuable asset with no payment!

What if all Christian spouses saw their marriage as being founded on Christ? What if they set themselves together on cleaning out the junk they have allowed to overwhelm their marriage with the help of The Master Renovator, The Holy Spirit? What if they ripped out the old and put up the new, then formulated a plan to fill the rooms up with the good stuff and not the bad? What if every spouse believed with all their heart that all their marital remodeling costs were already paid in full by Jesus Christ's blood on the cross?

The higher and deeper perspective to the aforementioned equestrian nightmare (pun intended) would include some of the following questions. Who let all the horses in? Why did we continue to allow all this mess to overtake our lives? The answer can be found in one word, disorder.

Relational Disorder slowly and steadily drains both spouses' Love Batteries, especially a wife's. To treat our marriage decently we need to inject it with godly order. Many families no longer function. They have gone off the rails. Chaos has become the new normal. Jesus Himself stated that the unchecked cares of everyday life and living will eventually produce spiritual weeds that choke out His will for the abundant lives and relationships He has designed for us to enjoy (Luke 8:14). Ordering our marriage provides both the weed control and the relational fertilizer needed for the landscape of our relationship to flourish spiritually, familially, financially, domestically, even nutritionally and physically. Each of these five areas of Relational Order can be considered a Battery Booster, in and of itself. Given that these emotional needs are closely interconnected, we chose to discuss them all in one chapter.

ORDER IN THE COURT

When most people hear the word "order" they initially experience either a few positive or a few negative thoughts. That is because every single person alive has a unique way of defining order and relating to order. This individualized subconscious view of order is shaped over a lifetime through numerous sources of conditioning, which include birth order, gender, family dynamics, occupation and brain structure. It is no wonder that countless views on the concept of orderliness create conflict in virtually every area of life and living.

To better understand godly order, it helps to examine ungodly order. God's order is not control or manipulation that serves the ego of a controller. It is not an arrangement of "do what I say, or else." God embodies Love (1st John 4:8). His type of love does not seek to control others, but rather to seek their good (1st Corinthians 13:5). Order is not a nagging wife screaming at her husband to clean the garage for the fiftieth time. It is not a husband who comes home and bullies his family to "keep them in check." Order is not religious legalism.

Godly order consists of vision, structure, teamwork, and God's grace to fulfill that vision. God says in His Word that without personal vision people's lives slowly decay (Proverbs 29:18). He also says that a party of two go nowhere together unless they are in agreement (Amos 3:3). Grace simply means you both have his unearned favor and divine ability to win at whatever you face together. Being heirs of the grace of life means that because you have His Holy Spirit in you, you will ultimately prosper in this life (1st Peter 3:7). He is on your side and you are on His. If God is for you and for your marriage, who can prevail against you (Romans 8:31)? As long as you pursue life in a loving way together, not turning against each other, there is nothing you cannot accomplish together for God.

It is important to see order through lenses of grace and not fleshly performance. If we simply pursue a list of daily "to do's" in order to feel better about ourselves, not having clear direction in our marriage, we will find ourselves on different pages in life and compare ourselves to others who seem to have more order. Seeing order through grace glasses results in you and your spouse coming boldly together to God's throne of grace, receiving His favor and ability to win together in whatever you put your hands to (Hebrews 4:16). You must both drop your performance issues at His feet and humble yourselves daily, operating exclusively from His favor and His ability in you. Then you must trust His ways, not your opinions or feelings (Proverbs 3:5-6). Most marriages don't follow this path. Why not be trailblazers?

SPIRITUAL ORDER

With God there is always a chain of command. Notice it is a chain of command, not a chain of demand. Order starts with God. God spoke and the universe came into order (Hebrews 11:3). We are spiritually made in His image (Genesis 1:27). Consequently we all spiritually desire order as well. Because of mankind's fallen nature our fleshly desires will always want to pull our lives either toward our own way of order or into complete disorder. Either of these paths takes us further from God's plan of order. We have the power and authority as believers to die to our fleshly disorder (Romans 6:11). Then we can live securely under God's loving order.

The order of The Church is presented to us in the Bible, with Jesus as the Head over His Church and all born-again believers collectively as the Body (Colossians 1:18). A physical body cannot function or coordinate without the electric impulses of the brain. You and I, The Church Body, must submit together to the leading of Jesus (Our Head) to coordinate in an orderly fashion to fulfill His Gospel mission to the world.

God created marriage to reflect Jesus' love for His Body of believers and the Body's response to that love (Ephesians 5:31-32). Men, think about that for a moment. If we draw all the love we need from our Head, Jesus, we can extend that love our wives and they will ultimately respond in some positive way. When I am at a loss on how to love Hollie, I go to Jesus to receive His kind of unconditional love. Then I know exactly how to love my wife in whatever state she is in.

The Word of God says that as Jesus is the Head of man, so a husband is head of his wife (1st Corinthians 11:3). That is not a popular statement today in secular America, but it is God's order for marriage. Most who disagree (including some Christian theologians) pick at semantics regarding definitions of headship and submission, pointing to overbearing religiously legalistic examples in society. They present a model of an ideal modern marriage in terms of equality. Both men and women are indeed of equal value, priceless to their Creator. Husbands and wives are to honor each other accordingly. The question is who is going to head up this God-ordained union? God's Word says this is the husband's role (Ephesians 5:23).

Christian husbands are to be the leaders in their homes. A man already knows if he is leading or if he is not. I tell men who don't lead that they already are the head, whether they feel like it or not. God created them to be so. They simply need to see themselves as such and step into their headship. Yes, it will take time. It will be an adjustment on everyone's part in the family. Some wives and children will resist. When a wife resists we should not force our way, even if we know that what we are asking is according to God's Word. Remember that God's love does not demand its own way. It is patient and not easily irritated (1st Corinthians 13:4-5).

HOLLIE'S HOTWIRE:
"As a wife, if you are the one leading, you are taking the position that was never designed for you. There is a reason your husband's shoulders are wider than yours."

In those moments of our wife's resistance, we as husbands need to stop and reflect on the areas of our own lives we had once not submitted to Jesus. We were resistant. Maybe we still are. Did we feel distant from Jesus? He never moved. We did. Did He stop talking to us? No, we just stopped listening. We stopped submitting. The Lord never pushes us away, even when we are stubborn. As born-again believers we are always His children, so we can always turn back to Him. When we do, He comes running for us. Remember the parable of The Prodigal Son? (Luke 15:11-32).

Also it is wise to see things from your wife's perspective. Be empathetic. She very well may have been used to carrying a spiritual mantle that neither fit her nor felt comfortable to her. Yet she felt she had to carry it. She may be afraid you will not continue to lead once you start. It may even be a bit confusing to her as to how to relax in her new-to-her role and give up the controls.

To be a godly head who ushers in spiritual order to the household, a husband needs to be a strong, loving, servant-shepherd-leader. Like Jesus is to him, so he is to be to his wife. Jesus was strong and passionate in loving us to the point of enduring the horrible death that brought us back into relationship with the Father (Philippians 2:8). He did not come to earth to be served, but to serve us and to give His life as a ransom for our freedom (Matthew 20:28). He leads and protects us, seeing the wolves at the door (John 10:11-12). Everything He tells us to be and do is for our good, even when He tells us "no."

The man who is that strong, loving, servant-shepherd-leader to his wife does not make any area of his marriage about himself. He will identify areas of selfishness and begin to die to them. He apologizes when needed, not out of shame, but out of a strong compassion for the love of his life to feel valued and encouraged. My pastor challenges men to begin to wholeheartedly "out-serve" their wives in the home. Husbands, it is time to lovingly and heartily take charge. As men, we tend to complicate headship instead of simply living headship. Just love your wife like Jesus loves you. And, yes, there is always room for improvement because we will always be growing in Christ over the span of our entire lifetime.

Husband, start to pray over your wife and marriage. After all, Jesus is your Intercessor (Romans 8:34). Open your mouth and start praying out loud regularly at the breakfast and dinner table. It doesn't have to sound pretty. It may seem awkward at first. Pray from the heart and begin to inject scripture into your prayers. God's Word is what will bring tangible results (Isaiah 55:11). Always pray by faith and in Jesus' name. Every negative situation will ultimately bow to The Name Above All Names (Philippians 2:10-11).

Both of you should always have your daily private connection with the Lord through praise, worship, Bible reading and prayer. Husband, you cannot effectively minister to your wife and children what you are not regularly receiving. Set aside a few minutes per week to share with your wife what God has been revealing to you and how He is changing you.

In addition to your daily individual time alone with The Lord, Hollie and I challenge you both to set aside 20 minutes together (at least once per week) for family worship. Make it like an abbreviated church service. Turn on a Christian themed Pandora or YouTube channel and worship God together during a song or two. Both of you put your total focus on God, setting your conflicts and cares to the side for the time being. Pray in the spirit, whatever that means to you (1st Corinthians 14:15, Jude 20-21). Then allow the Holy Spirit to guide you to a passage of scripture. Husband, read it aloud and apply it to whatever area of life the Lord would lead you to. Then both of you remain silent for at least a full minute to listen to God. Have your journals ready. You will know you are hearing from Him because His voice will always agree with His Written Word. Jot down what each of you hears from God. Then each of you share what God said. I cannot tell you the countless times Hollie and I have shared the same Word from His Throne Room, but in a different way. This type of regular spiritual connection together results in a deeper bond and clearer direction for your family.

Plug in at church together. If you both are not serving together at church in some capacity, begin to do so. I love seeing married couples ushering, greeting or serving in Children's Church together. The Bible says that out of love we should serve each other (Galatians 5:13). Attending church is not enough. When you serve at church, serve as to The Lord. Be sure each week to serve one service, then sit and receive together from the Lord in an additional service. Show up early, expecting to receive something powerful from God! Do not miss the first note of praise and worship. When our praises go up, the blessings come down. Don't make the mistake of believing that God only speaks during the sermon. The Holy Spirit will speak to you during corporate praise, but you have to be present to receive from Him.

Several things begin to happen when we make that quality decision to serve God at our church. We begin to connect with other believers, with whom we can experience mutual encouragement (Hebrews 10:25). As result, we become spiritually planted. God promises those who are planted in the house of God will flourish in all areas of their lives (Psalm 92:13-14). As we regularly serve we begin to operate in unity and fulfill our mission together to lead people to Jesus and mentor them in His ways (Matthew 28:19).

The most amazing thing that happens in the process of our serving is that we begin to discover and exercise our spiritual gifts. Hollie and I served in many of our church's ministries over the early years of our marriage. Some roles seemed to fit us and some did not, but we still served from the heart as to Jesus. We found needs and met them, regardless the task. As we approached serving in this way, the Lord began to funnel us more and more together into a type of effective stream which uniquely refreshed couples in our church. We could not put our finger on it at the time, but our Pastors began to recognize there was a special call for us. Our call carried spiritual gifting's that went beyond our natural talents.

In the world, Hollie had had an acting and production career of several decades. I had written three unproduced feature length screenplays. We had convinced ourselves that producing Christian Films together was our call in life. However, we never seemed to secure funding and did not have total peace on the matter. We felt as though we were banging our heads against the wall.

Our church's men's ministry at the time held their annual retreat. At the encampment, in a worship service, I told the Lord I was dumping my idea of how I wanted to serve Him. I asked Him how it was that He wanted to use me and Hollie for His purposes. At that moment my Pastor laid his hand on my head, declaring "this is a family ministry." At that moment the Holy Spirit opened my eyes to see that everything I had written in my scripts carried themes of restoration for marriages and families.

Upon returning home to Hollie, I told her I had news and for her to sit down. In the back of my mind I thought this might be the beginning of a major power struggle for the direction of our marriage. She had come to Los Angeles many years prior for the purpose of making a mark for Jesus in the Film and Television Industry. So had I. When I told her what God had revealed to me about us she giggled and said "no wonder I haven't booked any acting jobs since we married." She trusted me when I said I had heard from God and desired to followed His leading for our call. She trusted my headship.

Soon after, our Pastors asked to meet with us privately in our home. The Lord immediately told me that whatever they asked us to do to say yes. In the middle of them sharing their vision for home-based marriage enrichment groups, I interrupted and said yes. God empowered us at that moment for our call to take back marriage for Jesus. What you are reading and receiving in this book for your marriage is the fruit of two hearts that yielded to godly headship and submission. A marriage submitted to God becomes a powerful force for the Gospel.

What is the mission for your marriage? Do you feel you and your spouse have been running in one frustrating circle after the next? Do you feel that one emergency after another consumes your marriage? Do you find yourselves pulling at each other with your own visions for your marriage? If your marriage is plagued with double vision you will not see God's vision. God designed your marriage for His purposes. God has ordained a hope and a future for your marriage. The beginning of this future begins with His spiritual order of headship and submission. If you will both submit to God's roles for each of you, your marriage will gain traction and take ground for Him in a more effective way than you could have ever imagined.

FAMILIAL ORDER

A friend of mine once told me that when she and her husband were born-again she realized her 4-year-old daughter ran the family. By acting on godly wisdom her marriage gradually went from dysfunctional to flourishing. She and her husband took back their role as parents and began leading their children, who are both now ministry leaders in their church. Their children grew to be the influential adult leaders they are today because their parents took an active role in leading them.

Children grow spiritually, emotionally and socially when loving parents provide not only a supportive environment for them, but also a structured environment. Orderly kids absorb order, carrying it internally into every facet of adulthood. Those who grow up with little to no order tend to struggle more with spiritual identity, authority and even basic life skills.

If you grew up with any significant lack of family order, you can always learn to order your personal life. When I was a child, my father seemed so orderly to me around our home he almost clicked when he walked. I asked him once why he was so self-disciplined. He said he had always struggled with order because he had almost no boundaries as a child. All his physical needs were met. However, he could stay up as late as he wanted, get up when he wanted and eat anything he wanted at anytime. My dad was the youngest in his family. He was a good child and student. This may have been one reason my grandparents allowed him to self-govern a bit too much at an early age.

Dad raised my brother and me well. He was very involved in most every area of our family life. After college, he vigorously pursued his Masters Degree. By the time my older brother was in first grade, Dad was finishing up his Doctorate Degree in Theology while simultaneously pastoring a small church. In a time of self-reflection he found he had become obese and was a habitual nail biter. He took action to change in these areas so as to be an even better example for us to follow.

My father commanded respect in the home. He would let us go toe-to-toe with him with our opinions, but not to the point he would be disrespected. If we ever spoke to our mother disrespectfully he would immediately correct us in front of her. He listened to everyone's perspective on major family decisions, but ultimately made the final decision. Most of the time those decisions included some of all of the family's solutions. Because dad was always in charge, leading the way, we felt secure and actually had a lot of fun together. Dad laid the foundation for my brother and I to one day be the heads of our marriages.

Contrast my father's headship with how the world presents a husband's role. All you have to do is follow the thematic pattern of a husband in TV sitcoms since the 1970s. These shows often portray the man as bungling, lazy, irresponsible, lustful, and in charge of nothing. They present a love-starved, resentful wife as the one who "wears the pants." Much of American culture celebrates this backwards type of marriage. Many Americans have begun to imitate what the Entertainment Industry has distorted.

Men, never let your children demean or degrade you, even in a humorous way. Don't disrespect yourself to get a chuckle out of them. Kids need to have fun, but not the kind that downgrades your role as a parent. Do not let them hit you or scream at you. It is not good for you, or them, to allow them to cross your boundaries of respect. Otherwise, their respect for authority outside the home will not be intact. They eventually will suffer the consequences. It will also negatively affect their future relationships.

If you have no children in the home, guess what? The two of you are a family. You still need order. Sit down and have a weekly 15-minute meeting together to coordinate your schedules. Husbands, initiate this meeting. Try using Day-Timers, or something similar. I am more effective with a printed organizer than with simply entering appointments into my smartphone calendar. My organizer helps me to be more efficient and productive, as it gives me more of a comprehensive view of where I am headed and why.

When Hollie and I began to have our weekly 15-minute meetings we realized how backed up we were in managing our lives together. We thought we were running in the same direction, but in reality we were on different tracks. As a result, our first meeting ended up taking well over an hour. After a few weekly meetings, the time lengths gradually reduced closer to the 15-minute mark. If we waited longer than a week to reconvene, we found the amount of time required for the next meeting stretched out significantly longer.

Meeting on the fly (while showering, driving or performing household chores) will create more miscommunication and miscoordination. Utilize your time together in places like the car and the kitchen exclusively for Simple Conversation. To have an effective meeting you must sit alone together, with no distraction, so you can hear and completely understand each other regarding your schedules.

One item that must be entered into your itineraries is the day and time of your next 15 minute meeting. Also write down the dates, locations and times of your weekly date night, as well as your twice-per-week time for lovemaking. If you have children in the home, plan a separate short meeting twice per month as a family. That way you will all literally be on the same page. When you act as a family according to a written schedule, peace is ushered into your home. Your children are more secure.

What I like about entering my life into my Day-Timer is that I don't have to try to remember so many things. I am not left with the anxiety of wondering if I am where I need to be, or if I have forgotten a meeting. It is all written down. It is a budget for my time. Dave Ramsey has a financial budgeting app called Every Dollar. His motto is to make every dollar count. What if we were to value our time like we valued our pocketbooks, making every hour count.

FINANCIAL ORDER

Speaking of Dave Ramsey, have you noticed in recent years how popular his books, financial seminars and podcasts have become? I believe the reason for this is that most families' finances are spiraling out of control. This is happening within all walks of life. As a whole, Americans are heavily in debt, with no effective plan to get out (and stay out) of debt. Many middle-aged adults see no hope for a decent retirement. Most families are underfunded in (or have no) emergency savings. This has resulted in many people working ridiculously long shifts for years on end with little sleep. This rat race was never God's plan for us. He desires for us to financially prosper and to be physically healthy, not just for our souls to spiritually prosper (3rd John 2). Overwork can lead to long-term illness and spiritual weariness. As a result, we can even be tempted to emotionally check out on our spouses and family. We can develop a distorted identity. We can even begin to feel disconnected from God.

You might be reacting to what I a just said with something like, "well, what else can I do? I have to work like crazy, or I and my family will sink!" My answer to you is in the form of a three-part question. Do you and your spouse operate together off of a pre-agreed, written, joint, monthly budget? If so, does this budget consist of more than a handful of line items? Finally, if either one of you has not faithfully adhered to a comprehensive budget (allowing your money to spend itself) how would you expect you would handle the additional income? The answer to the third question is that you wouldn't.

The solution to most financial dilemmas is not necessarily to immediately get another job. The Bible says if you are faithful over little you will be ruler over much (Matthew 25:23). God also says to whom much is given, much is required (Luke 12:48). If you and your spouse are not budgeting every dollar you both are currently making, you are not ready to take on more income. Your dollars would leak through your fingers like water. You would wonder where it all went. We must all learn how to truly budget and be in agreement together over our financial plan before pursuing another job or taking on extra overtime shifts. If you press forward without a plan for your money, your marriage will likely suffer. You will be like a ghost floating in and out of your home. There is nothing wrong with working harder, but with this bootstrap approach to getting ahead financially it would be wise to also work smarter; smarter, meaning within the freedom of an adequate budget.

Notice I said "the freedom", not "the confines" of a budget. When we choose to operate regularly from a budget, which accounts for every dollar, we don't have to think about where our money is going. Each dollar has already been assigned a predetermined destination. Because of this your brain is set free from worrying about whether or not you have forgotten a bill, have enough cash for your son's new track shoes, or if you've socked enough away for your spouse's upcoming birthday gift.

When I was single I thought that the five items I had written on a legal pad constituted an actual working budget. Nowhere on this legal pad were there categories for groceries or fuel. I typically had

$300.00 or less in emergency savings. Of course I raided these savings just about every week for none other than groceries and fuel. Since I defined groceries as any kind of food, I spent these unbudgeted dollars on dining out (which I did 75% of the time). I was also spending upwards of $120.00 per month on Starbucks Carmel Macchiatos. As a result of my reckless spending habits, I was living well beneath what my income level could have afforded me.

When I got engaged to Hollie, she had already completed a 13-week Dave Ramsey Financial Peace University Group. She had more personal finance knowledge than I did at that moment. I knew that as the future head of our marriage I needed to lead in our finances. I immediately read one of Dave's books to get myself to buy into his plan. I also attended a two-hour introductory FPU workshop. I had Hollie download some of Dave's budgeting forms for me to immediately begin to flesh out the kind of budget I had never had before. Four months into our marriage Hollie and I completed Financial Peace University together.

Hollie and I have never fought about money. We have more than enough emergency savings. We have a Last Will And Testament, as well as enough term life insurance on each other to ensure that neither one of us would be financially burdened in the event of the other's passing. It grieves us every time we see people asking for help with burial costs on a Go Fund Me social media page.

Through following Ramsey's Seven Baby Steps to Financial Peace we are now completely debt free, except for the balance on our home mortgage (which we will soon begin to pay off early). Not only do we tithe to our local church, we budget for regular giving to other ministries. Because of this, God has been faithful to His Word in opening the windows of heaven to the extent we have an even greater abundance to give even more (Malachi 3:10).

My former approach to money had been under-informed, bordering on childish. God's Word says that when we were children we thought, spoke and acted as children (1st Corinthians 13:11). Now that we are grown we must act as adults, including within the financial realm. God proclaims that His wisdom shouts loudly in the streets (Proverbs 1:20). Sound, godly, practical, workable financial answers are screaming in your face right now! Gather that knowledge immediately and act on it. Acting on sound knowledge is the very definition of godly wisdom. Hollie and I highly recommend that after you have finished The Love Battery, that together you both seek out a financial plan that will get you on the same page with money. Of all the plans we have explored, Ramsey's has proven to be the most practical, effective and rewarding for us. His website is www.daveramsey.com.

DOMESTIC ORDER

We all have our strengths and weaknesses in marriage. I will admit that tidiness and household organization have been some of my weaker areas in regard to meeting Hollie's emotional needs. Over the years I have gotten better at it. Someone once told me that they believed household teamwork to be defined as each family member doing only those things they are good at. But what if most of the family declare themselves only good at a very few tasks, leaving the bulk of the housework to one person because "that's their thing?" This is neither fair nor efficient.

In this material we will define Domestic Order as coordinating with your spouse and children in the overall maintenance of the home, including the exterior property and all possessions housed within it. Everyone must contribute in several ways in order for this need to be met. Too many naive husbands think that simply mowing the yard and changing the oil in the car fulfills their domestic obligation. This philosophy leaves too many a frustrated wife resenting her husband and children, as they pursue their hobbies and she slaves away at the remaining 90% of never-ending indoor chores. Husbands, it's time to wake up and not just smell the proverbial coffee. It's time to brew it. Seriously, if she's the one that brews your coffee, start beating her to the coffeemaker each morning and brew it for her. An entire book of the Bible was named specifically for this exclusive male duty. It's entitled "He-brews!"

Domestic Order is mainly about all the little things. It's when the little things are ignored that they turn into bigger things. To prevent this negative buildup we would do well to stop making chores out to be so dreadful and complicated. Start with, for example, making the bed. Whichever one of you it is that needs to step up their game in the Domestic Order arena, make your bed first thing when you get out of it. U.S. Naval Admiral William H. McRaven, who oversaw the Navy Seal Operation that killed Osama Bin Laden, challenged University of Texas college graduates in a commencement speech to make their beds with a higher purpose in mind. He said "if you make your bed every morning, you will have accomplished the first task of the day. It will give you a small sense of pride and will encourage you to do another task, and another, and another. And by the end of the day that one task completed will have turned into many tasks completed." He went on to say "if by chance you have a miserable day, you will come home to a bed that is made (that you made!). And a made bed gives you encouragement that tomorrow will be better. So if you want to change the world, start by making your bed."

Jesus instructed a paralyzed man to take up his bed and walk (John 5:8). He could have told him to leave that nasty old mat of affliction on the ground and to not look back. But the newly healed man would have needed that bed each night, so he packed it away in some semblance of order. Perhaps Jesus advised this individual to pick up his mat in order to jumpstart his new chapter of health with a new healthy habit. Start a new small orderly habit of your own today. God says that you are who you think you are (Proverbs 23:7). Begin to see yourself as an orderly person. Act on your new self image daily in little ways, then in bigger ways. This will help you to gain momentum on the domestic front.

Husband, as the head, take the lead and ask for a meeting with your wife regarding Domestic Order. Discuss and agree on a vision of how you both would like your home to ultimately look. Get creative. Cut out some magazine photos and create a Domestic Order Vision Board. Then formulate a plan together as to how you and the family can help this vision to become a reality. Each of you take out your Day-Timers. Divide up tasks and enter them into your weekly calendars. Share the plan with your children, advising them on their responsibilities to help fulfill the vision. Examine your Domestic Order Plan once per month in one of your weekly 15 Minute Meetings. Scrap what does not work. Expand on what does.

You may be at the point of needing to hire some outside help for your home. After two knee surgeries I realized it was no longer wise for me to climb the slope in my back yard to pick weeds. We employed a landscape company for a nominal price to maintain both the front and back yards on a weekly basis. Now that Hollie and I are over the age of 50, we are considering hiring a cleaning person. Stooping to scrub showers and clean toilets could quickly result in chiropractic bills exceeding what we would pay a maid!

Enjoy the fruit of your household labors. Have a candle-lit dinner on your immaculate patio. Declare a movie night in your clutter-free master bedroom. Soak in a steaming bubble bath, as you breathe in the clean smells of a spotless bathroom. The ongoing reward of consistent Domestic Order will be an enriched soul (Proverbs 13:4).

NUTRITIONAL & PHYSICAL ORDER

As born-again believers, our bodies are a holy dwelling place for the Holy Spirit (1st Corinthians 6:19). We are to bring honor to God in the way we nurture our health. The computer science acronym GIGO stands for "Garbage In, Garbage Out." The GIGO principle implies that bad input into a computer will ultimately produce a bad output. Just as a computer program requires specific data for it to respond in a productive way, so our bodies need the right kind of nutritional fuel for us to function properly in all areas of life and living.

Nutritional and Physical Order are necessary in marriage for multiple reasons, including consistent vitality and for being physically attractive to your spouse. The Apostle Paul says that when a man loves his wife it is evidence that he loves himself (Ephesians 5:28). We must love ourselves in order to fully love our spouses (Mark 12:31). Many people don't think too much about loving themselves by taking care of their health.

71

Exercise plays an important part in our health. However, the problem has been that too many Americans have leaned too much on the gym and not enough on a balanced meal plan, supplemented with vitamins and minerals. Many nutritionists are taking the stance that overall health and weight management are effectively achieved primarily through 80% nutrition and 20% exercise.

Many people believe that simply eating a low fat diet and taking vitamins A through E promotes a healthy disposition. Unfortunately, this is far from being true anymore. Many decades ago Americans were able to get most of their vitamins and minerals through the vegetables and fruits grown on their own property. The soil back then was packed with almost all the nutrients needed to live a long, healthy life. The farm animals people owned were not plumped up with hormones or antibiotics. The food these edible animals were fed was not genetically modified. I believe my Grandmother, who lived to 103, built up her basic constitution and resistance to disease early in life by consuming mainly the beans, tomatoes, onions, carrots and peas she grew in her garden.

Today it is a different ecological story altogether. Regardless of produce that is advertised as being grown organically, we can no longer depend on the soil it was grown in to pass on to us the essential minerals we need for maximum health. Our ground in the U.S. has not been nutrient rich for almost 100 years. For that reason we must all take quality mineral supplements. Dr. Joel Wallach, author of the book Dead Doctors Don't Lie, insists that all humans require at minimum 90 essential minerals in order to stay vibrant and resistant to disease. He even shares documented cases of people reversing many so-called incurable diseases through regular doses of specific minerals.

We all should eat mostly lean proteins, along with generous portions of non-starchy vegetables and some fruit. Cut out as much processed food as you can possibly think of, especially bread and cereals. Most processed food contains gluten, which basically consists of grain proteins that act like glue to hold the shape and texture of food. If you cut out sugar and gluten from your diet, you will lose weight almost immediately. You will also quickly lose inches around your waist, being as most of what we consider to be belly fat is actually toxic inflammation. This inflammation we carry eventually becomes a breeding ground for many diseases. Scary, right?

We should also be drinking much more water than we typically do. To calculate how much daily water you need, take your current weight in pounds and divide it by two. The resulting number should be the amount of water in ounces you should be drinking each day. For instance, if you weigh 150 pounds you should drink a total of 75 ounces of water per day. Sometimes when our bodies are dehydrated, we perceive it as hunger. We think we need sugar or a protein snack, when what we really need is water. Water can better energize us for longer periods of time than caffeine. You'll be visiting the bathroom quite a bit more, but the benefits of proper water consumption will far outweigh the slight inconvenience.

If I were to tell you that Hollie and I followed our meal and supplement plan 24/7 I would be lying. We are foodies. We have agreed we will eat according to our plan, faithfully taking our Youngevity brand supplements, six days a week. For one meal per week, mostly on date nights, we choose to deviate from our Nutritional Order and consume whatever we want. We have coined this feeding of our appetites as a weekly "mercy meal." We don't use the term "cheat meal" because we are planning it, not trying to get away with something. When we do get off track with our weekly nutrition plan, we simply get back on it again.

When it comes to exercise find an activity you enjoy, preferably together. For many, that activity might simply be walking together on a regular basis. For others, that could be swimming a few laps in the pool or bike riding together. Pick up the pace a bit. Have goals. Be sure to stretch. Enter your time for exercise into your calendar until it becomes a habit.

Ushering order into our marriages and families reduces the effects of stress, opens our souls up to God's rest, and gets our families operating as a team to undertake and complete the mission the Lord has predestined for our lives. Our steps are ordered by the Lord. He delights in our steps when they are in lockstep with His (Psalm 37:23). Take the first step toward order in one area of your life, even if it is a baby step. Little by little you will produce more and more fruit in all areas of your life together. Then watch the combined power of your two Love Batteries take you for the ride of your life. You will not be disappointed. I guarantee it!

PLUG IN

1. Together, in pencil, fill in the Relational Order Worksheet found in APPENDIX H. Prayerfully form and shape your calling as a family over the weeks ahead. Print out your family scripture and family mission statement. Display it in a place where the entire family can read it often and declare it out loud. Begin to draw your marital identity from it.

2. All of us can improve in the area of Financial Order. If you are not operating together from a successfully proven financial plan, find a plan you both agree on and immediately begin to act on it. We highly recommend Dave Ramsey (www.daveramsey.com).

3. Have a weekly fifteen-minute meeting together to coordinate your schedules. At some point in your meeting enter the date and time of next week's fifteen-minute meeting, as well as your weekly date night and the two times you will make love.

ZAPPLICATION NOTES

CONCLUSION

Charging Forward

When it comes to charging each other's Love Batteries, it is
important to remember that it is not about perfection. It's about
direction. I was with Hollie at a local shooting range when she fired
a rifle for the first time. I had given her prior instruction on how to
hold and aim the firearm. Her target was set thirty yards out. She had
had a rough workweek, so her arms were tired. As a result, when she
first lifted the rifle she began to shake. Suddenly the man next to her
began to fire his huge handgun, inadvertently raining hot casings
onto her. He soon realized what was happening and moved. Hollie
lifted her gun again and shot ten rounds. Upon retrieving the target,
we were amazed to find that all of her shots at least hit the paper.
Some of them even came very close to the bullseye. I was so proud
of her for pushing past the resistance, from within and without, and
coming so close to hitting her mark on the first try! That same paper
target hangs on the wall of our home office to this day.

Hollie and I challenge you in the same way to forget your past
failures and press to hit the mark of God's high calling for your
marriage. You won't hit the romantic bulls eye every time, but
because your spouse will know you are aiming for it they will feel
loved. We urge you to periodically revisit the chapters of this book
that have most helped you in sharpening your marital skills. Be
patient and gentle with yourselves and with each other. God loves

you both so much. He is always on the side of your marriage. He will give you the ability to love each other like He loves you.

We invite you both now to take the Battery Booster Identifier Questionnaire (BBIQ), found in APPENDIX I. This will help each of you to rank your greatest emotional needs, so that you and your spouse can begin to charge each other's Love Batteries on a regular basis.

Ladies and gentlemen, your engines are started. Your batteries are charged for the long haul. There are quite a few laps ahead. The checkered flag is waving you on. Let's ride!

APPENDIX A

WHEN YOU DO (OR SAY), I FEEL…

Write five negative one-word feelings and five positive one-word feelings. Remember that negative feelings are not bad. Feelings can be used for feedback. Do not take your spouse's feelings personally. Own your own feelings.

Positive: Negative:

1._____   1._____

2._____   2._____

3._____   3._____

4._____   4._____

5._____   5._____

Read the guidelines from the Simple Conversation chapter for using the WHEN YOU DO (OR SAY), I FEEL tool. Now practice expressing these one-word feelings to your spouse by plugging them into the following phrase:

"When you_____, I feel_____.

This phrase, when used properly, can solve up to 90% of your conflicts.

APPENDIX B

CONFLICT RESOLUTION WORKSHEET

1. Pray together.
2. Make the following commitments together. One of you read them out loud:

A. We commit to be positive throughout our discussion.
B. We will avoid the "A.D.D.'s." We will not give into unharnessed ANGER, become DEFENSIVE, or DWELL on each other's past mistakes.
C. If the negotiations seem to not be getting anywhere, or if one of us begins to show any signs of the A.D.D.'s, we will stop and come back to the table later (preferably by day's end).

3. Agree upon and write down what the conflict is in two sentences or less.

4. Each of you write down your individual thoughts and feelings regarding the conflict.

5. One at a time each of you share your thoughts and one-word feelings by using the phrase "when you do (or say), I feel." While your spouse speaks, jot down a few notes on what they're saying. Repeat each other's thoughts and feelings to each other to ensure you both clearly understand each other.

6. Each of you write down as many of your individual solutions you can think of.

7. Share your individual solutions with each other. Select portions of each of your solutions that you are BOTH enthusiastic about. In this way you join your individual solutions to form a RESOLUTION. Read the resolution to your conflict out loud.

Our Resolution together is:

8. After an agreed-upon period of time, evaluate together how well your resolution is working. If effective, continue with the current resolution. If not, go back to your individual solutions to form a new resolution together.

ROMANCE ACROSTIC

Starting with each of the following letters, write down seven Romantic Gestures that help you to feel romanced (i.e. the letter "**O**" could signify "**O**pen my door).

R-

O-

M-

A-

N-

C-

E –

Now switch worksheets with your spouse. Circle two Romantic Gestures you will demonstrate on a regular basis.

APPENDIX D

ROMANTIC CHARGING POINTS & SHORT-CIRCUITS WORKSHEET

ROMANTIC CHARGING POINTS - list a few specific behaviors that your spouse does to help you feel romantic.

- _____

- _____

- _____

ROMANTIC SHORT- CIRCUITS - list a few specific behaviors that your spouse does that kill a romantic moment.

- _____

- _____

- _____

Switch worksheets with your spouse. Circle two Charging Points and two Short-Circuits that you will consciously include in (or eliminate from) your daily behavior toward your spouse. Have your spouse briefly elaborate on the impact these behaviors have on their ability to feel romantic.

APPENDIX E

Date Night Planning

Each of you list two types of date activities you would enjoy doing within each category.

Level 1	Free Date	Wife:_____
		Wife:_____
		Husband:_____
		Husband:_____
Level 2	$15.00 Date	Wife:_____
		Wife:_____
		Husband:_____
		Husband:_____
Level 3	$50.00 Date	Wife:_____
		Wife:_____
		Husband:_____
		Husband:_____
Level 4	$75.00 Date	Wife:_____
		Wife:_____
		Husband:_____
		Husband:_____

Enter a weekly date night into your family calendar, incorporating these activities.

APPENDIX F

**FAMILY VACATION AND "JUST THE TWO OF US" GETAWAY
DREAMING AND PLANNING WORKSHEET**

It is wise for you each year to have both a family vacation AND a separate
vacation (or getaway) just for the two of you. Fill in the following categories of
vacation dreams together. Be as specific as possible about the activities you wish
to engage in during these vacations.

OUR FAMILY VACATION DREAMS
(8 to 12 months from now)

OUR "JUST THE TWO OF US" GETAWAY DREAMS
(8 to 12 months from now)

OUR BIG TICKET FAMILY DREAM VACATION
(2 to 4 years from now)

OUR BIG TICKET "JUST THE TWO OF US" DREAM VACATION
(2 to 4 years from now)

REGULAR SEX POP QUIZ

1. Lack of sex in marriage is a valid excuse for infidelity.

True/False

2. According to an Ohio State research study of college-aged young adults, it was estimated that a man has close to 19 sexual thoughts per day to a woman's_____.

A. 2 sexual thoughts per month
B. 2 sexual thoughts per day
C. 5 sexual thoughts per day
D. 10 sexual thoughts per day
E. None of the above

3. Fulfilled desire promotes continued desire, which minimizes _____ desire.

A. Increasing
B. No
C. Straying
D. Sexual
E. None of the above

4. Numerous scientific studies agree that regular sex occurring at least _____ helps husbands and wives to stay healthier and more vibrant.

A. Twice per week.
B. Twice per month.
C. Once per week.
D. Once per month.

5. The benefits of regular sex include:

A. Higher levels of a blood protein that fights viruses.
B. Potential lower blood pressure.
C. Increase of a woman's vaginal moisture.
D. Cutting a man's likelihood of heart disease in half.
E. All of the above.

6. Regular sex promotes higher levels of oxytocin, a hormone that contributes to an emotional state of_____.

A. Anticipation
B. Ecstasy
C. Bonding
D. Empathy
E. C and D only

7. It is helpful and biblically acceptable for married couples to view graphic sex instructional videos together.

True/False

8. For a man to learn consistent ejaculatory control, it is best for him to_____.

A. Relax his pelvic area
B. Always be on top
C. Regulate his breathing
D. All of the above
E. A and C only

9. If a woman does not have an orgasm at some point during lovemaking, she is not truly enjoying herself.

True/False

10. We can effectively combat depression through _____.

A. Continuing to have regular sex
B. Confessing personalized scripture verses (by faith) out loud in our private time.
C. Serving consistently as a church volunteer.
D. Regular personal worship.
E. All of the above.

ANSWER KEY

1. False

2. D

3. C

4. A

5. E

6. E

7. False

8. E

9. False

10. E

APPENDIX H

RELATIONAL ORDER WORKSHEET

I. Family Mission Statement:

II. Family Scripture:

III. Roles together (to fulfill your mission).

    1.

    2.

    3.

    4.

    5.

    6.

    7.

    8.

IV. Fill in the above Family Mission Statement, Family Scripture and your combined roles together. Fill in the chart on the next page with the prioritized roles, along with Weekly Time Estimates. Jot down regular activities that relate to each role. Add up all the time estimates for a weekly total. Weekly estimates, based on a 15 hour day, should total no more than 105 hours. There are 168 actual hours in one week. An Example Worksheet and Chart have been included as a reference.

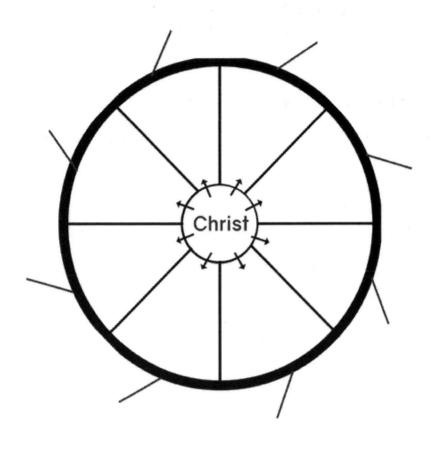

RELATIONAL ORDER WORKSHEET AND CHART
(EXAMPLE)

I. Family Mission Statement: Blessed as a family to be a blessing.

II. Family Scripture: Of Him, through Him and to Him are all things. Romans 11:36

III. Roles together (to fulfill your mission):

      1. Spouses

      2. Parents

      3. Household Money Managers

      4. Church Volunteers

      5. Extended Family Members

      6. Personal Evangelists

      7. Employees

      8. Knitter (her) / Soccer Player (him)

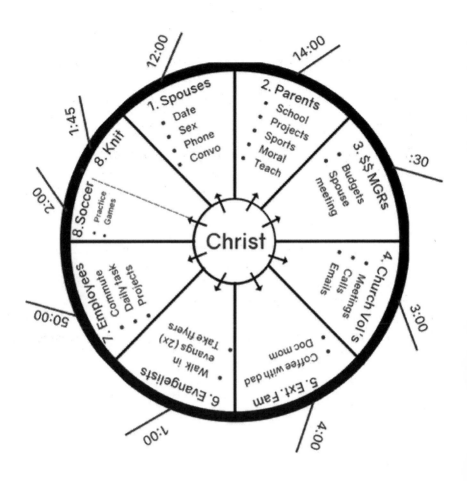

Battery Booster Identifier Questionnaire (BBIQ)

1. When daydreaming, I might find myself thinking mostly about_____.
A. Something erotic.
B. Something witty that was said that made me laugh.
C. Something fun we can do together as a family.
D. What else I might be able to mark off my "to do" list for the house.

2. I would feel the most disappointed if my spouse_____.
A. Forgot what I had told them I wanted for my birthday.
B. Spent over the family budget on a costly personal item.
C. Gained enough weight in a couple of months to go up a pants size.
D. Returned to a behavior we both had agreed The Holy Spirit told us to stop.

3. At the end of the day I would feel most satisfied if my spouse would_____.
A. Make love to me.
B. Sit and listen to the good, bad and ugly of my day.
C. Engage with me (and the kids) in one of our favorite hobbies or pastimes.
D. Spend 5 minutes cleaning a disorganized room.

4. I would feel the most fulfilled if my spouse_____.
A. Gave me a decent massage.
B. Went with me to a personal finance seminar.
C. Took a brisk walk (or jog) with me.
D. Committed to daily personal worship, prayer and Bible study.

5. I wish my spouse would _____ more often.
A. Initiate sex.
B. Ask me how I am feeling.
C. Declare a family game night.
D. Cook a meal or wash dishes.

6. My spouse could score the biggest love points with me
by_____.
A. Leaving a "just because I love you" personalized greeting
card in the car for me to find when I leave for work.
B. Balancing the checking account.
C. Taking time to prepare a healthy lunch bag for work that
does not include fried food or candy.
D. Reading the Bible together with me at least once per week.

7. When I feel overwhelmed by life and living, my spouse
could help me feel appreciated by_____.
A. Having a make out session with me on the couch that
would eventually lead to the bedroom.
B. Listening to my issues without offering solutions.
C. Helping the kids with a class project.
D. Cleaning out the cat litter box, brushing the dog, or
watering the plants.

8. I would feel the most offended if my spouse_____.
A. Stood me up on a date.
B. Spent what was budgeted for our electric bill on daily trips
to the coffee shop.
C. Stopped taking vitamins and mineral supplements for an
entire month, resulting in illness and missed work.
D. Said they needed a two-month break from church.

9. It would hurt me the most if my spouse were to_____.
A. Deprive me of sex for a month.
B. Give me the silent treatment for three days because they were angry with me.
C. Be a no show for an important family event.
D. Leave all the household chores to me during the work week, while they engaged in social media.

10. The thought of _____ really excites me:
A. A night on the town, alone with my spouse.
B. My spouse I and working together on a plan to be debt free.
C. My spouse and I preparing lean, gluten-free meals for the week.
D. Serving together at church.

11. Sometimes I want to scream_____.
A. "Let's have sex already! I'm dying here!"
B. "We don't really talk anymore!"
C. "Will you please connect with our child?! They need you!"
D. "Will you please help me around the house for once!"

12. When we were dating, I felt ____ when my spouse ____.
A. Special, when they surprised me with my favorite food.
B. Secure, when I found out they had an emergency savings account to last them a few months.
C. Attracted, when they reached a body weight (or exercise) goal.
D. Impressed, when they showed up early for church.

13. After a satisfying day, I would remember how my spouse_____.
A. Made love to me, even though I knew they didn't feel like it.
B. Gave me their full attention when I was speaking.
C. Sat down to make plans together for a family vacation.
D. Made the bed or made breakfast for us.

14. I feel irritated or hurt when_____.
A. I don't hear "I love you" at least once per day.
B. It's the end of the month and there's not enough money for groceries or gas.
C. I see my spouse regularly filling up on fast food.
D. See my spouse slipping out of their faith into fear or depression.

15. I would most want my spouse to ask me_____.
A. "What can I do to please you tonight in bed?"
B. "What's your perspective on what we're talking about?"
C. "What can we do together that will help us connect as a family?"
D. "What can I do to help prepare the house for company this weekend?"

16. Complete the following sentence. "Honey, what I really need from you right now is to _____."
A. "Hold me."
B. "Pay off the credit card. Better yet, cut that card up!"
C. "Drop the Twinkie and slowly step away from the pantry!"
D. "Stop and worship The Lord with me for a few minutes."

17. I feel the most loved after_____.
A. A mutually satisfying sexual experience.
B. A respectful, equal exchange of ideas and thoughts.
C. My spouse informs me the children have completed their homework.
D. The car has had the oil changed and the gas tank is full.

18. When I feel close to my spouse, I am more inclined to_____.
A. Reach out and grab their hand.
B. Consider ways I can help us build a better financial future together.
C. Slim down a bit, in order to look more like I did when we got married.
D. Notice specific ways they are growing spiritually and compliment them on it.

19. One of the main reasons I married my spouse was_____."
A. For sexual fulfillment.
B. For emotionally connected communication.
C. To be a godly, thriving family together.
D. To be a productive team together that would take good care of the material possessions God would bless us with.

20. The quickest way to my heart is through _____.
A. Non-sexual touch.
B. Finding a bargain.
C. Making health-conscious choices together.
D. Praying with me.

BBIQ Answer Key & Prioritizer

1. Make a mark after each answer you chose for both odd and even numbered questions.

Odd numbered answers:
A.
B.
C.
D.

Even numbered answers:
A.
B.
C.
D.

2. The letters below correspond to the 8 Battery Boosters with which your spouse can best charge your Love Battery.

Odd Numbered Answers:

A. Regular Sex - engaging in mutually satisfying sex with your spouse on a regular basis at least twice per week.

B. Simple Conversation - privately engaging in mutually satisfying everyday communication, where both parties feel understood and both are free to express themselves openly in a respectful way.

C. Familial Order - working together to maintain a family structure that helps children to develop spiritually, mentally, emotionally and socially.

D. Domestic Order - coordinating with your spouse and children in the overall maintenance of the home, including all possessions housed within it and the exterior property.

Even Numbered Answers:

A. Romantic Gestures - affectionate acts that demonstrate care and promote emotional connection.

B. Financial Order - acting according to a mutually agreed-upon financial plan.

C. Nutritional and Physical Order - maintaining a physically pleasing appearance (and vibrant disposition) through proper nutrition and supplements, as well as regular exercise.

D. Spiritual Order - acting according to Biblically assigned marital roles, with the husband as the strong, loving servant-shepherd-leader and the wife as the one who freely submits to him. Every team needs a leader!

3. Rank your Battery Boosters numerically, from highest to lowest, based on the number of marks you made for each answer.

__ Simple Conversation

__ Romantic Gestures

__ Regular Sex

__ Spiritual Order

__ Familial Order

__ Financial Order

__ Domestic Order

__ Nutritional & Physical Order

4. Now switch papers with your spouse. Circle their top 3 Battery Boosters. Write them down in a place you can easily access (i.e. sticky note, smartphone). Review these needs each morning. Plan ways to meet their needs in a way that helps them to feel loved. Get regular input from each other on how boosted your Love Batteries are percentage-wise. Periodically ask each other "what can I do to fully charge your Love Battery?" Have fun!

ABOUT THE AUTHORS

Kurt and Hollie Bryant serve as Elders and Marriage Ministry Leaders at Elevate Church in Newhall, California. Their mission together is to take back marriage for Jesus through God's love and wisdom. Since 2013 they have helped to equip hundreds of pre-engaged, engaged and married couples with valuable relational tools to assist in living the most satisfying and rewarding relationship that God has established on earth, MARRIAGE. The Bryants reside in the Los Angeles area. If you would like information on forming marriage enrichment groups in your church, utilizing The Love Battery book as curriculum, feel free to contact them at thelovebattery@gmail.com.

91604542R00060

Made in the USA
San Bernardino, CA
23 October 2018